Guitar Picking Tunes
CLASSICAL GEMS

by William Bay

To access the online audio go to:

WWW.MELBAY.COM/30872MEB

The 714ce-N guitar on the cover is courtesy of Taylor Guitars.

© 2020 by Mel Bay Publications, Inc. All Rights Reserved.

WWW.MELBAY.COM

Preface

This book contains guitar arrangements by Mel Bay, Ray Bell, Mike Christiansen and yours truly on some of the most beautiful and famous music ever written. Featured are composers such as J. S. Bach, Beethoven, Schubert, Schumann, Tchaikovsky, Vivaldi, Debussy and more. The works span the musical eras from the Renaissance through late Impressionism. All the pieces are presented in notation and tablature. An online audio recording of each piece is included. (Both steel and nylon string guitars were used on the recording.) These guitar solos can be played in concert, recital or just for enjoyment. I hope you enjoy this treasure of great music carefully scored for pick-style guitar solo.

William Bay

Index of Solos

Title	Page	Audio
Adelita (Tárrega)	28	16
Acadian Melody	70	36
Ballo Francese (Manierio)	8	3
Barcarolle (Coste)	15	8
Bourée (J. S. Bach)	6	2
Canon in D (Pachelbel)	30	17
Chanson Triste (Tchaikovsky)	21	12
Chorale (Schumann)	26	15
Clair de Lune (Debussy)	22	13
Dolores (Waldteufel)	10	5
Etude (Mozzani)	38	21
Etude in A Major (Sor)	12	7
Für Elise (Beethoven)	18	10
Gavotte (J. S. Bach)	42	23
Gilotte (Renaissance Dance)	9	4
Gymnopedie (Satie)	32	18
Harpsichord Dance (Scarlatti)	11	6
La Paloma (Yradier)	66	34
Lágrima (Tárrega)	20	11
Largo (Vivaldi)	69	35
Meditation (Massenet)	50	27
Menuet (Quantz)	56	30
Minuet (J. S. Bach)	4	1
Minuet (Krieger)	55	29
Moonlight Sonata (Beethoven)	40	22
O mio babbino caro (Puccini)	16	9
Pavane pour une infante défunte (Ravel)	37	20
Prelude (Weiss)	24	14
Prelude in B Minor (Sor)	52	28
Prelude in C Major (J. S. Bach)	62	33
Serenade (Schubert)	58	31
Study in D Major (Sor)	46	25
Study in D Minor (Tárrega)	48	26
The Girl with the Flaxen Hair (Debussy)	60	32
Traumerei (Schumann)	44	24
Valse (Durand)	34	19

Minuet

J. S. Bach
arr. by Ray Bell

Bourée

J. S. Bach
arr. by William Bay

Moderato ♩ = 104

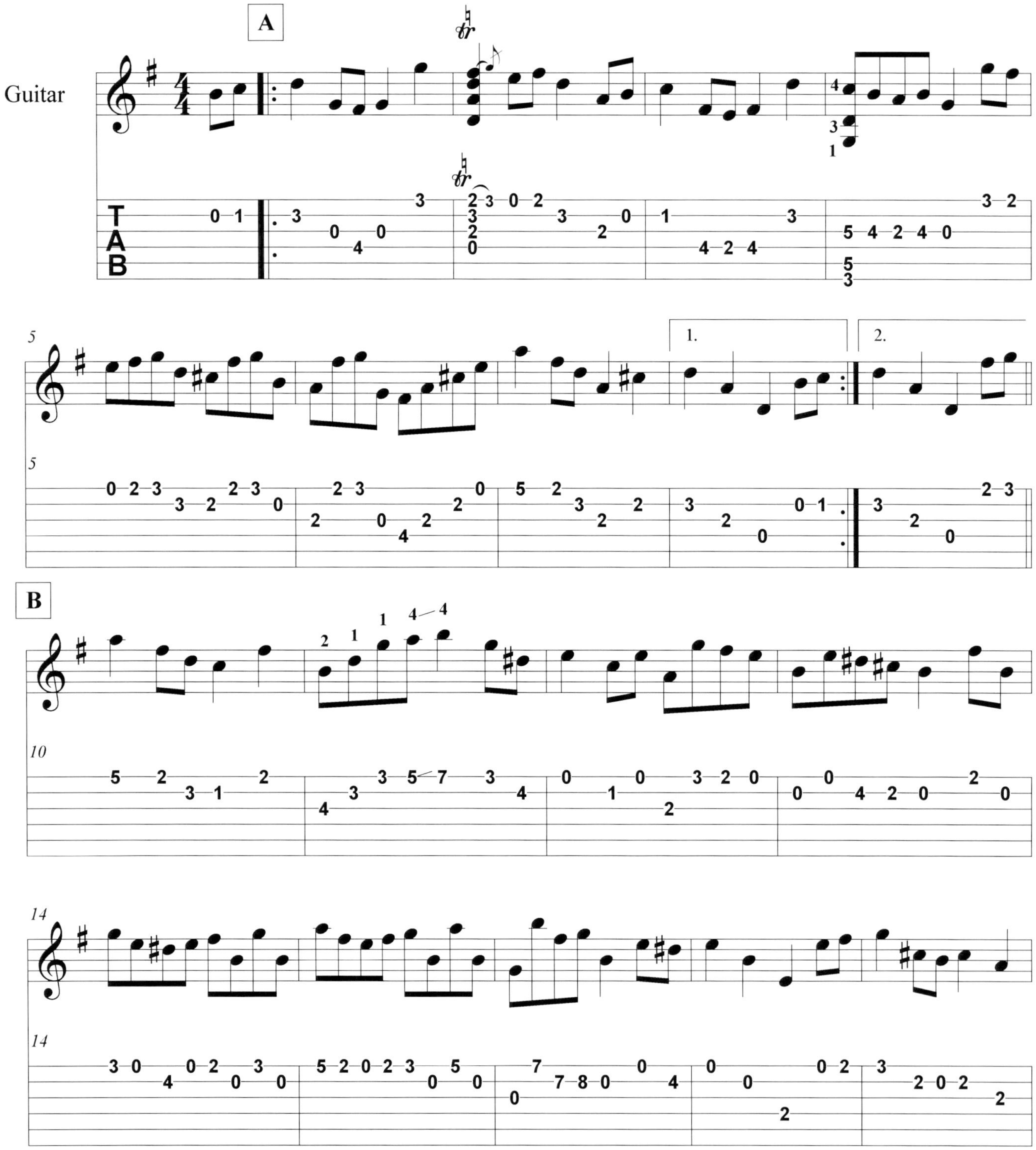

Ballo Francese

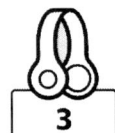

Capo 3rd Fret for a higher key

Don Giorio Manierio
arr. by William Bay

Gilotte

Renaissance Dance
arr. by William Bay

Moderato ♩ = 120

Dolores

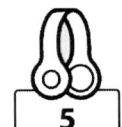

Waldteufel, Op. 170
arr. by Mel Bay

Dropped-D Tuning

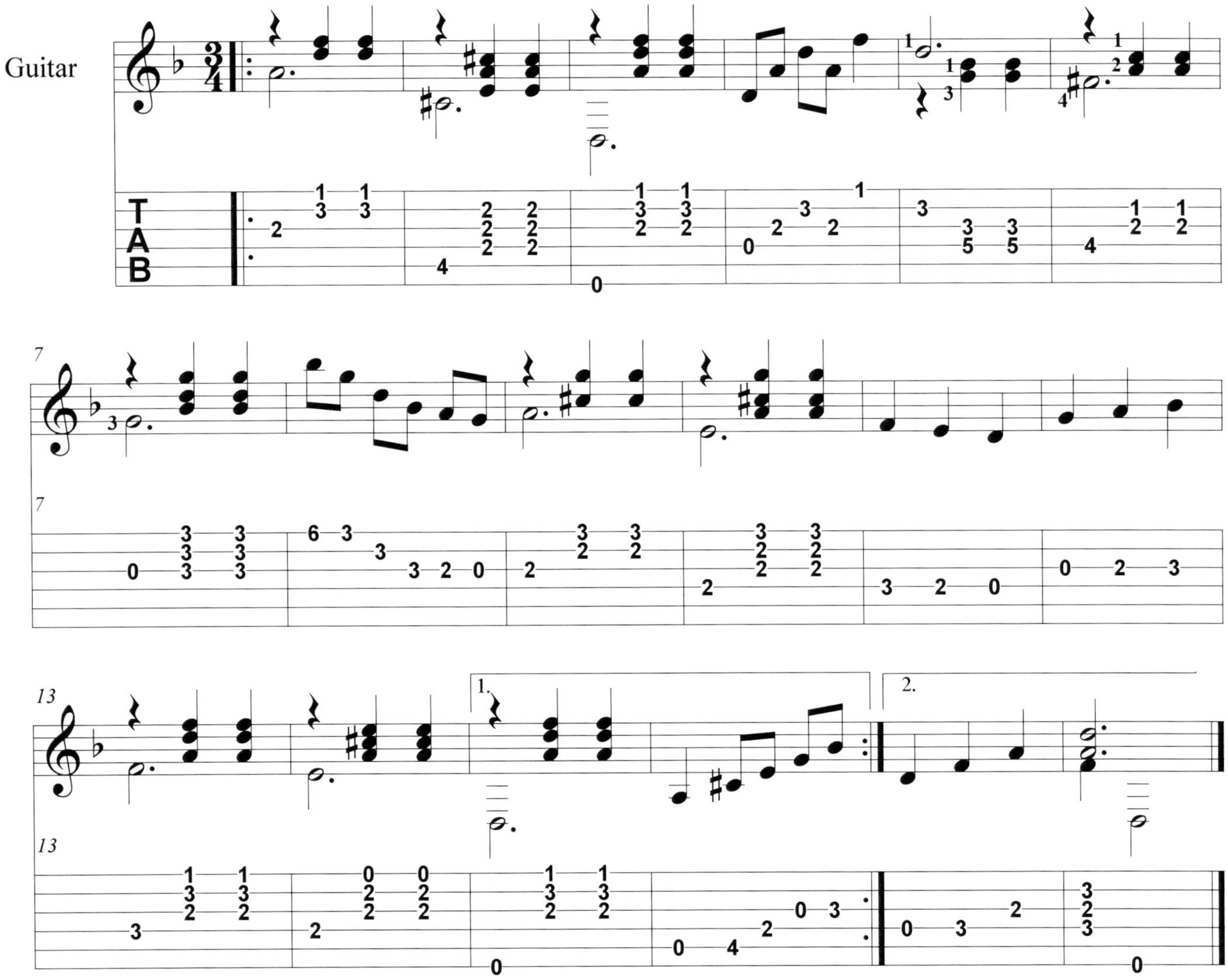

Harpsichord Dance

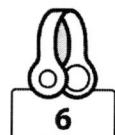

Domenico Scarlatti
arr. by Ray Bell

Dropped-D Tuning

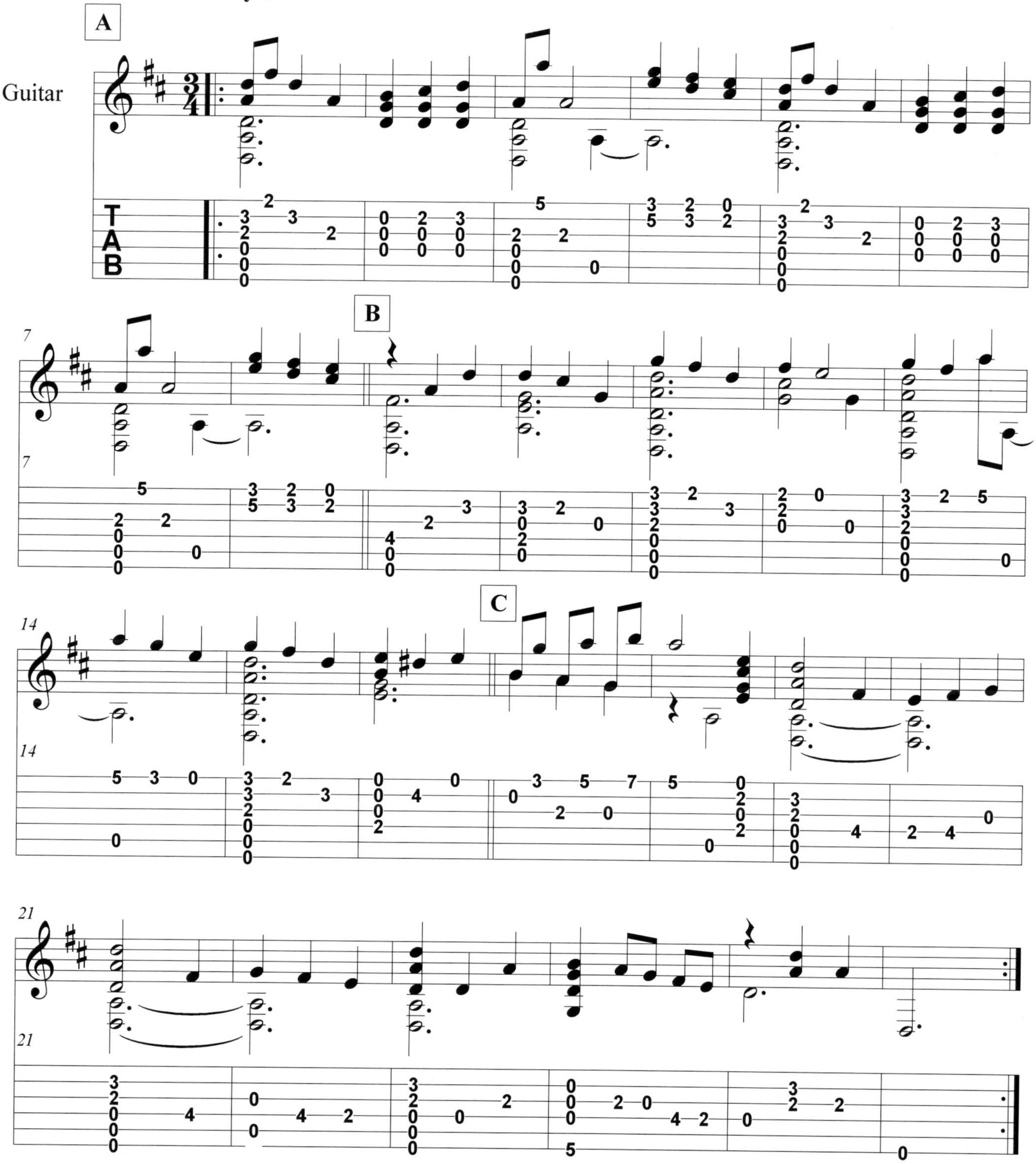

Etude in A Major

Sor
edited by William Bay

Andante ♩ = 48

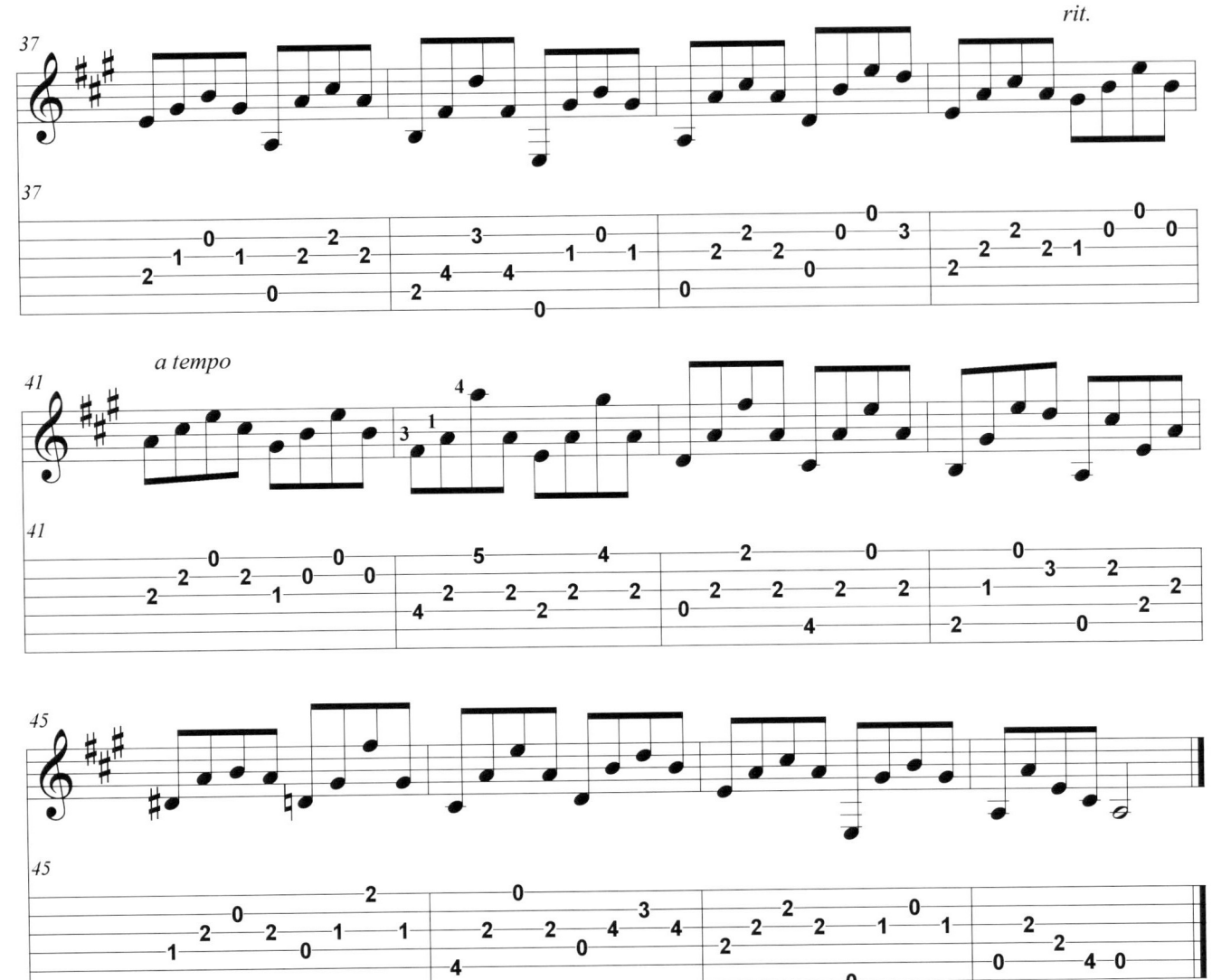

Barcarolle

Napolean Coste
arr. by William Bay

Andante ♩ = 74

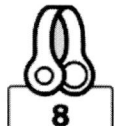

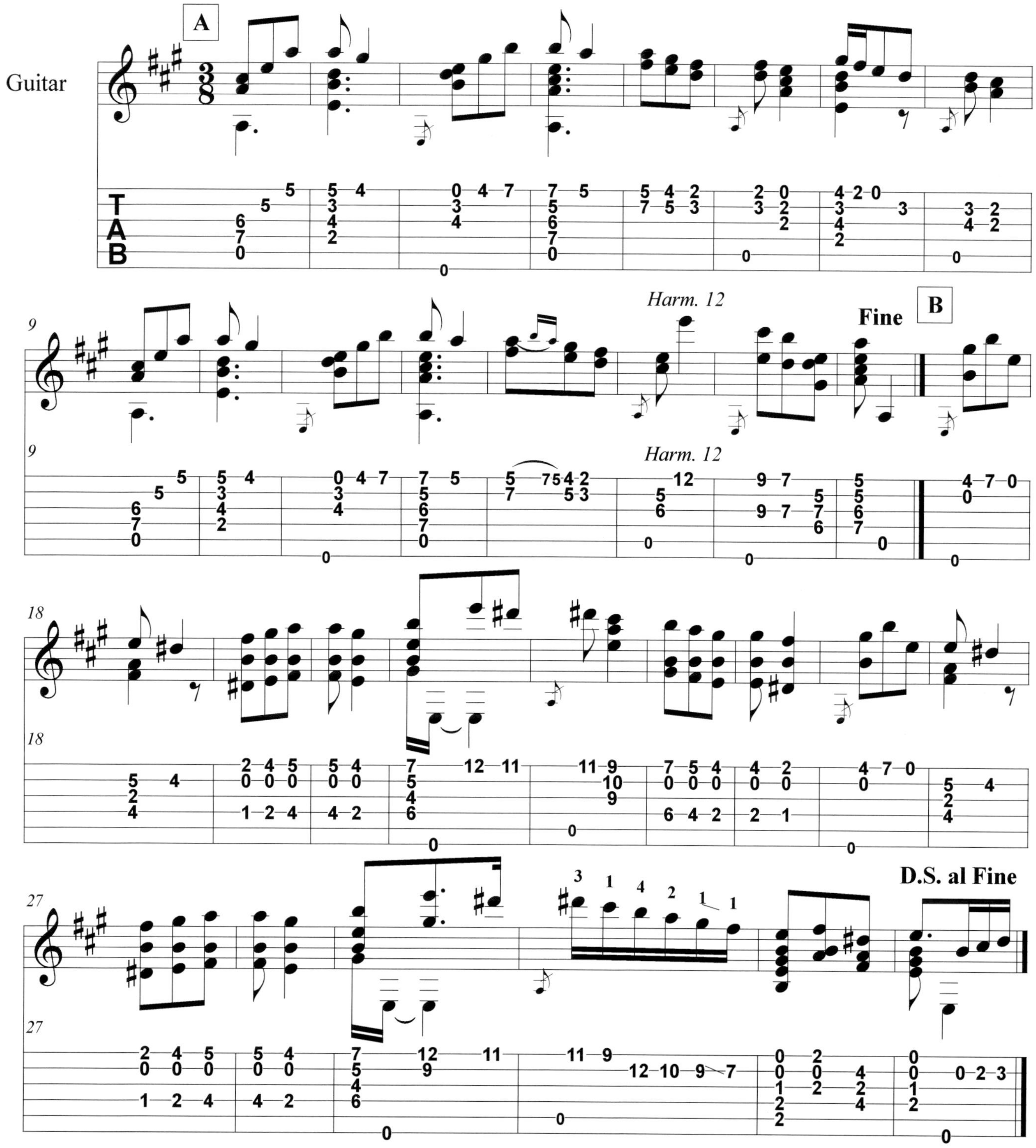

O mio babbino caro

Giacomo Puccini
arr. by Mike Christiansen

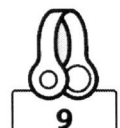

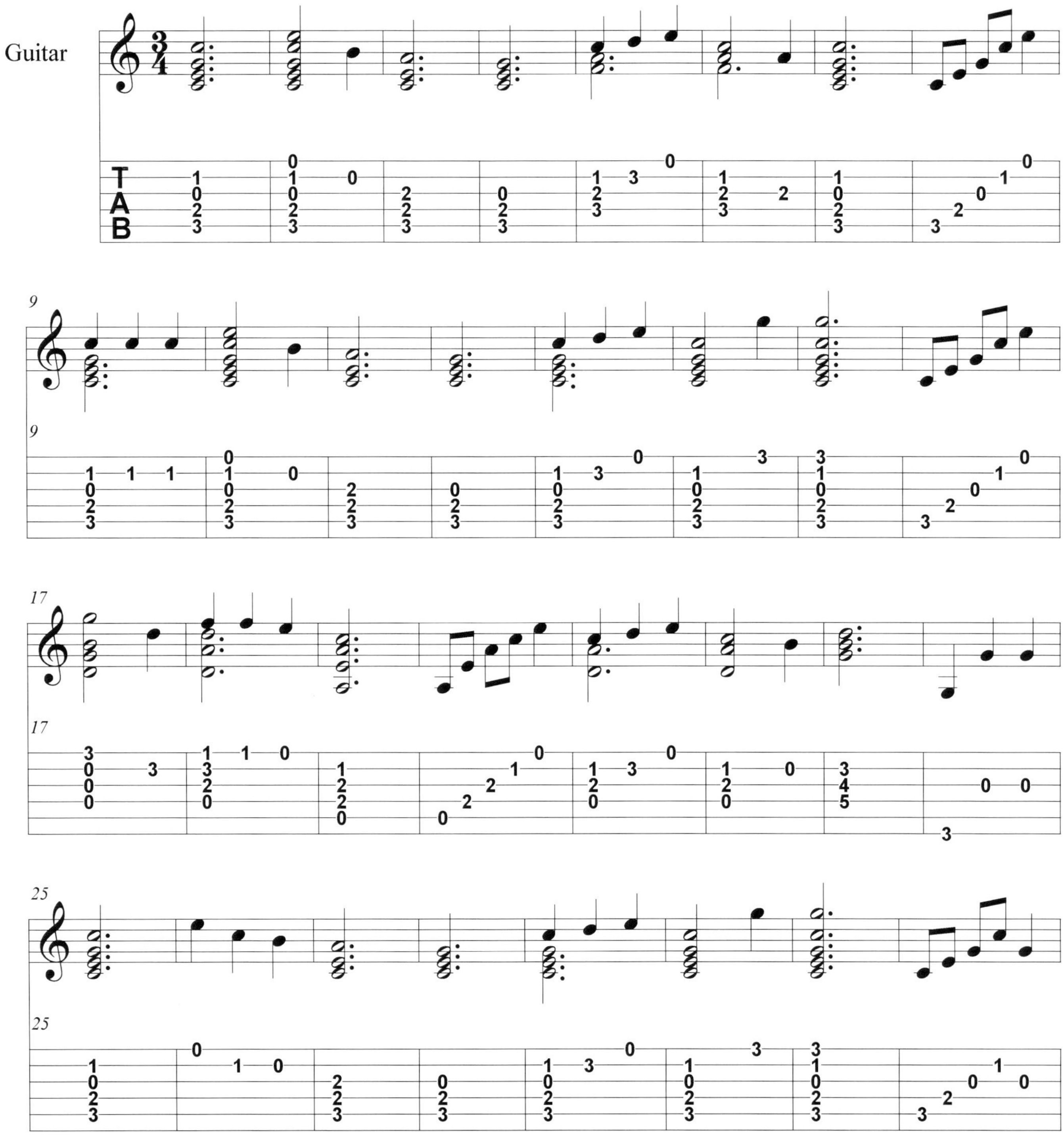

Für Elise

Beethoven
arr. by William Bay

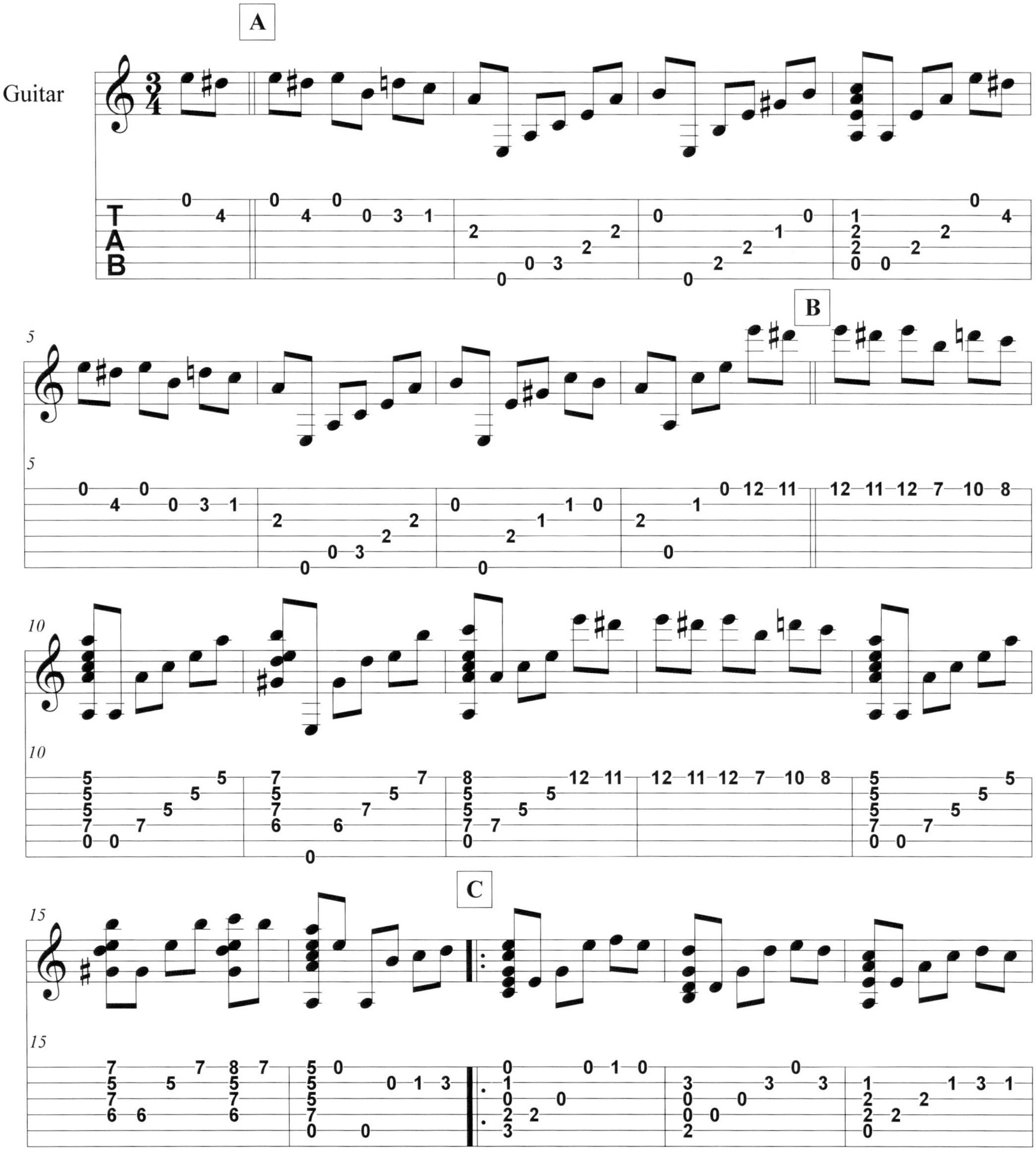

Lágrima

Francisco Tárrega
arr. by William Bay

Andantino ♩ = 76

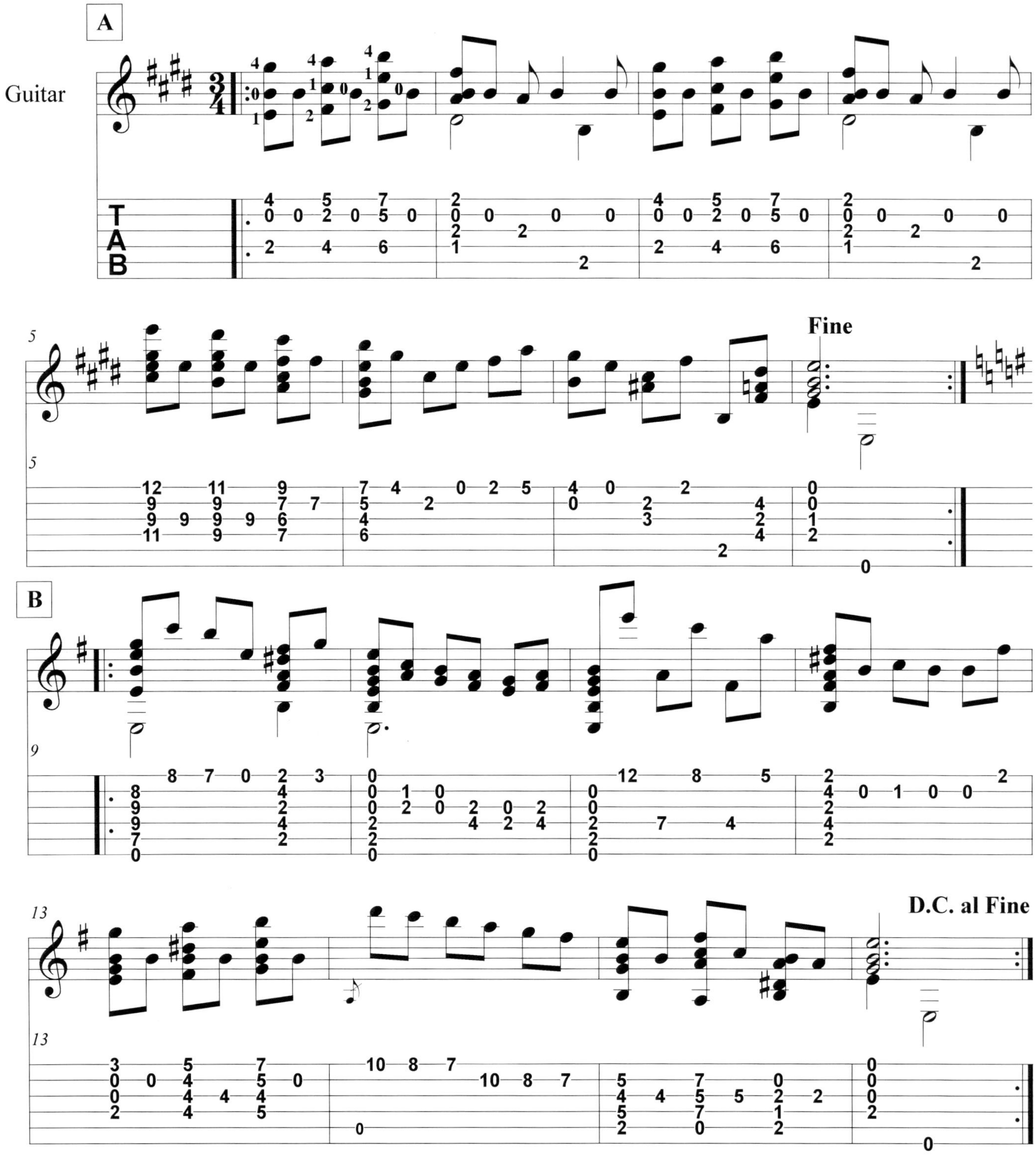

Chanson Triste

Tchaikovsky
arr. by William Bay

Clair de Lune
Theme

Claude Debussy
arr. by Ray Bell

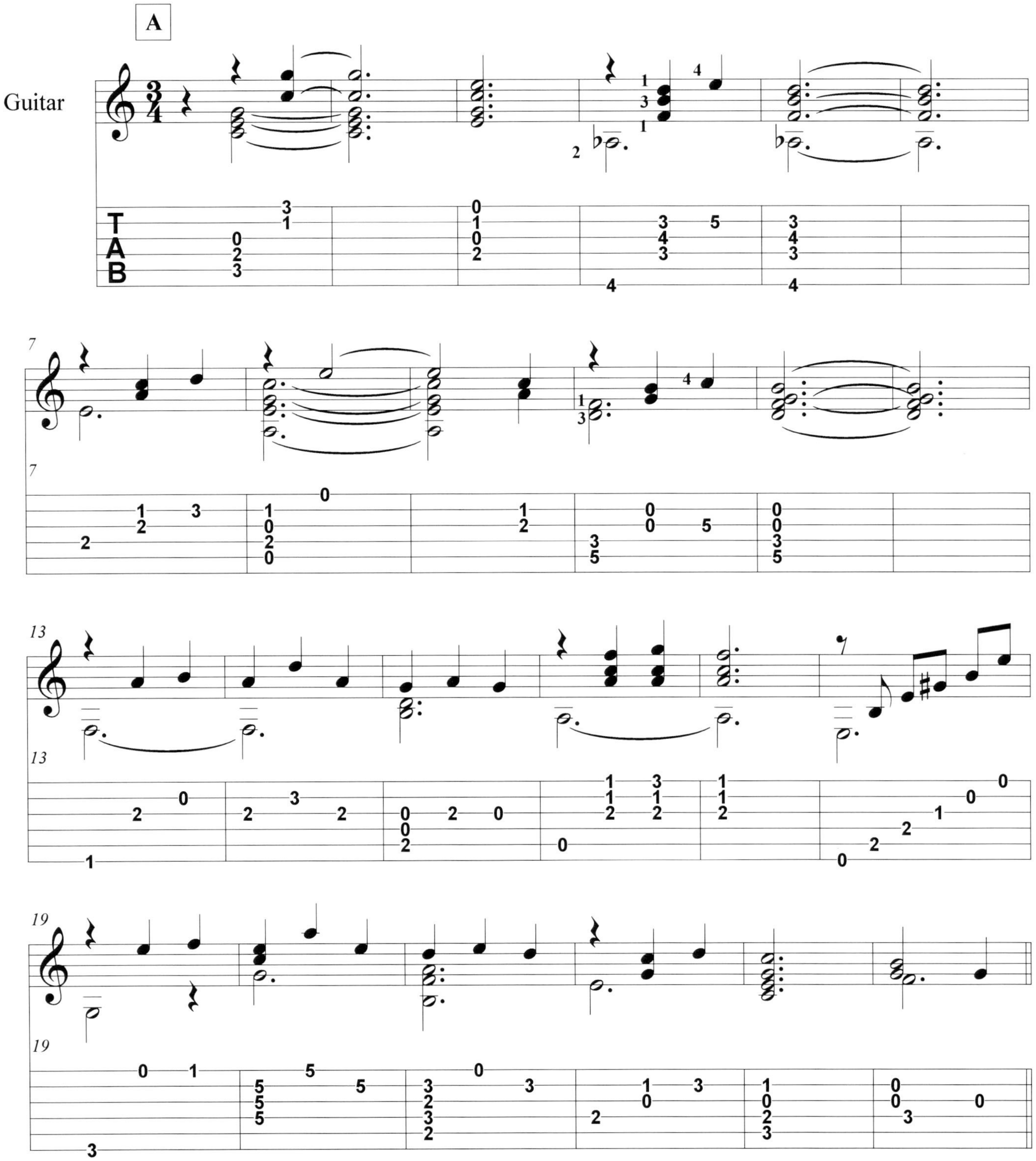

14

Prelude

Silvius Leopold Weiss
arr. by William Bay

Freely, with expression ♩ = 80

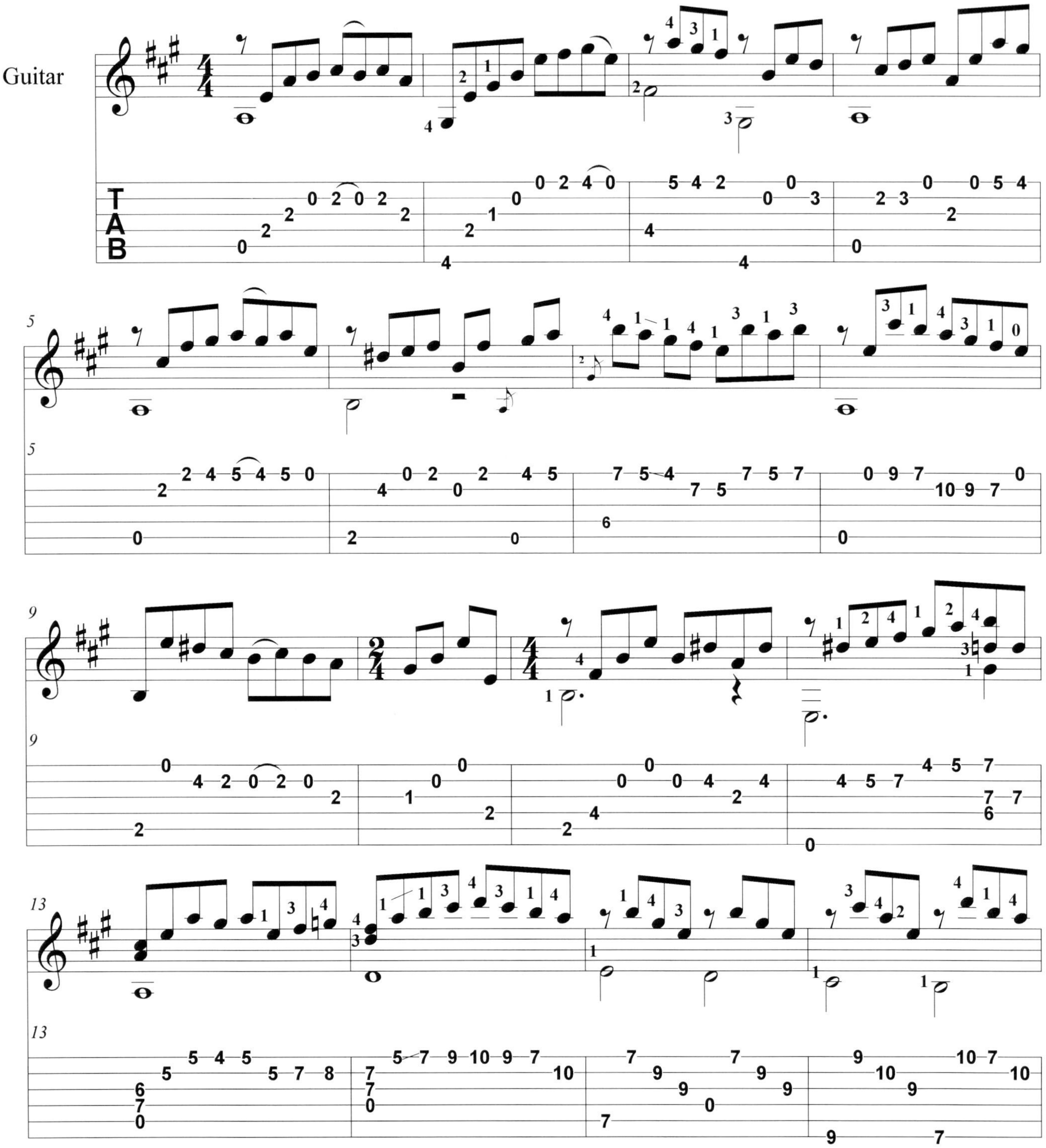

Chorale

Robert Schumann
W.B. based on an arr. by Ray Bell

Dropped-D Tuning

Andante ♩= 68

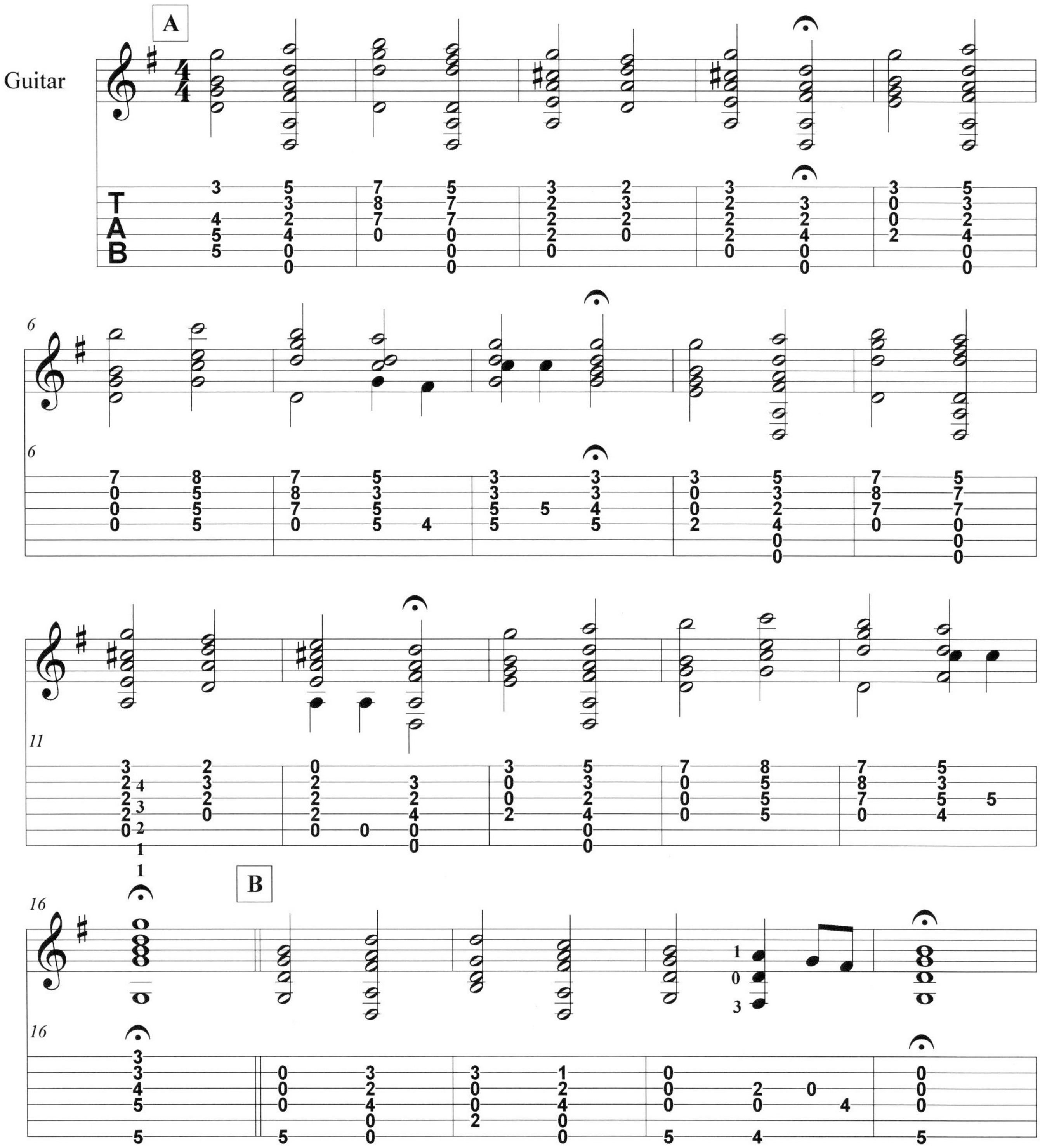

16

Adelita

Francisco Tárrega
arr. by Mel Bay

Andantino ♩ = 84

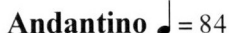

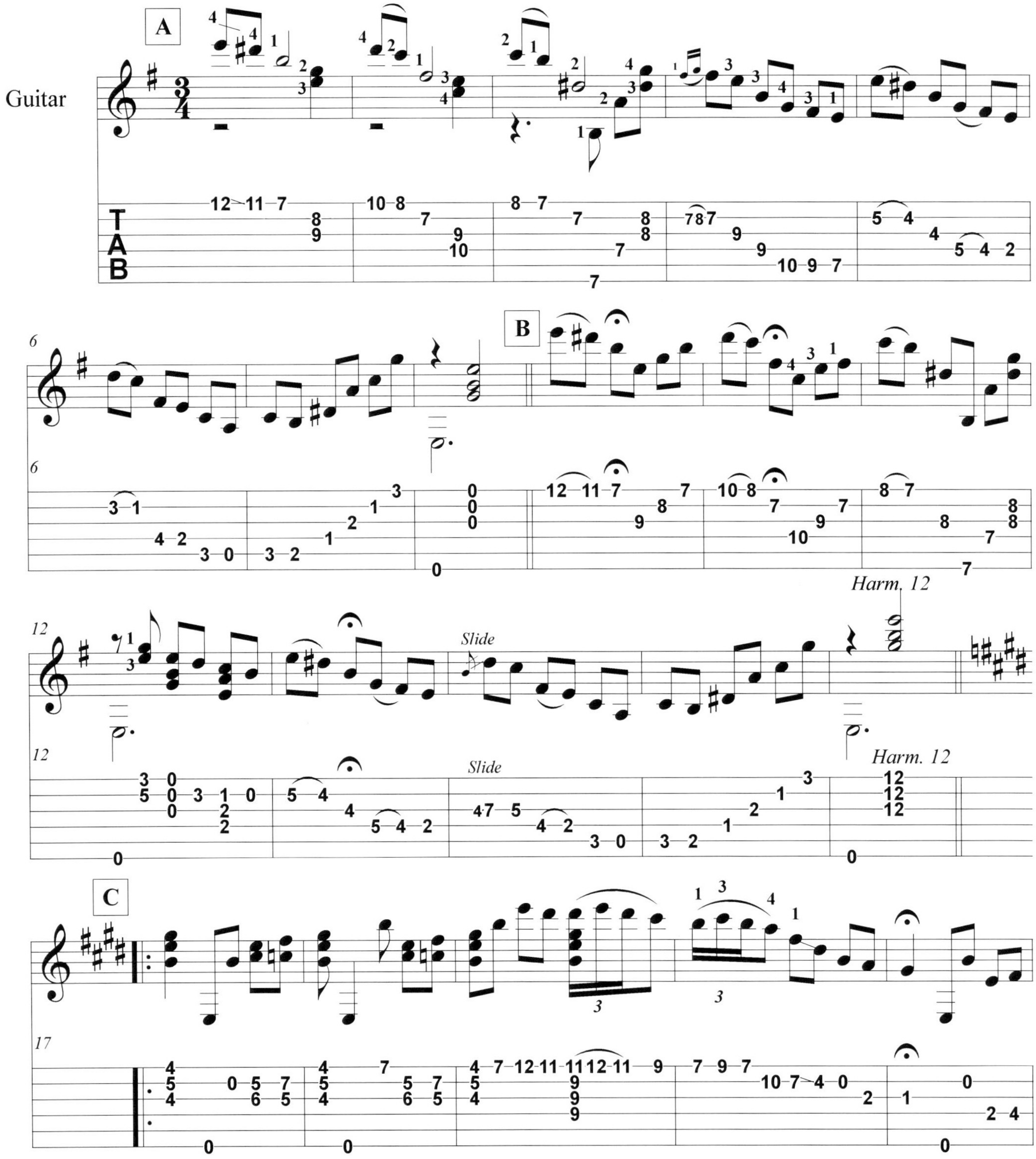

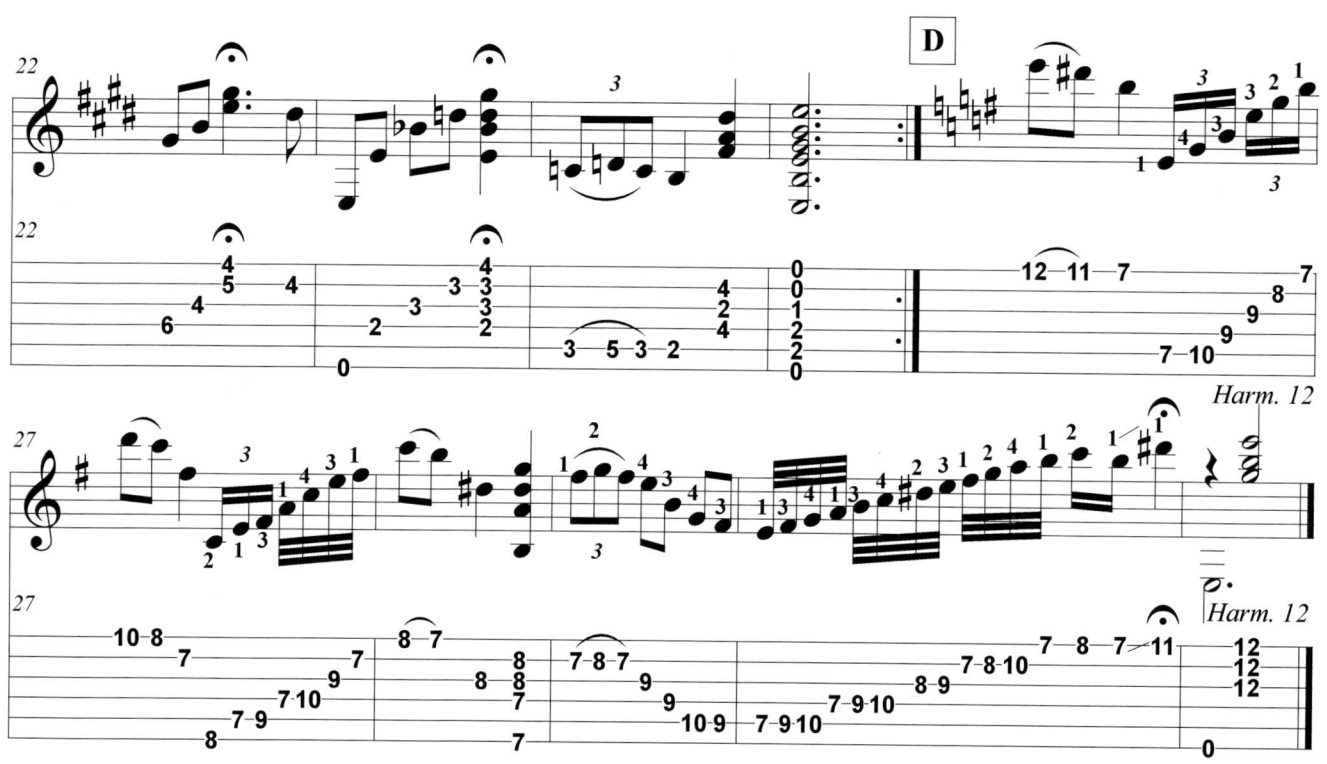

Canon in D

17

Pachelbel
arr. by Mike Christiansen

Moderately slow ♩ = 72

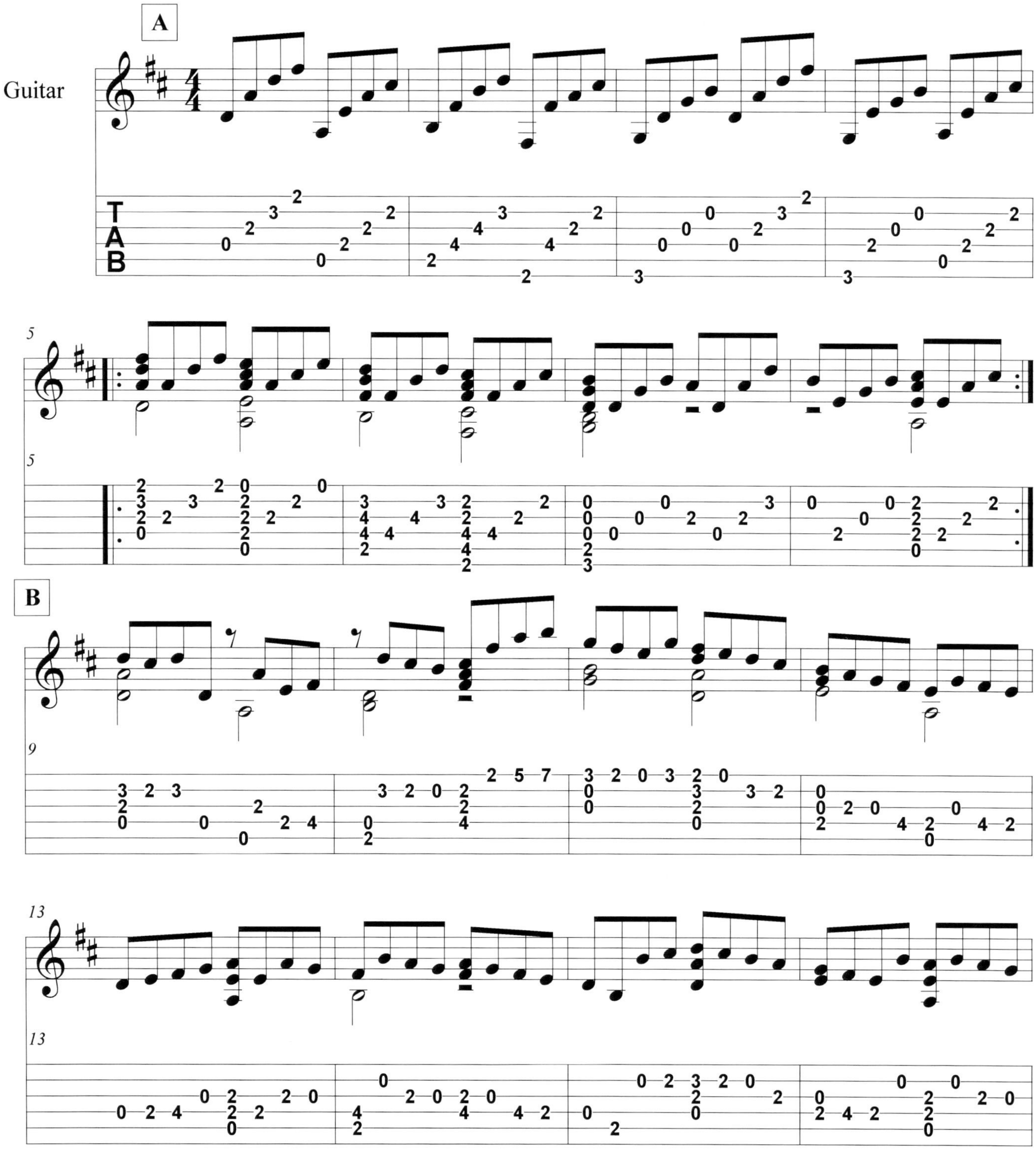

Gymnopedie

Eric Satie
arr. by Mike Christiansen

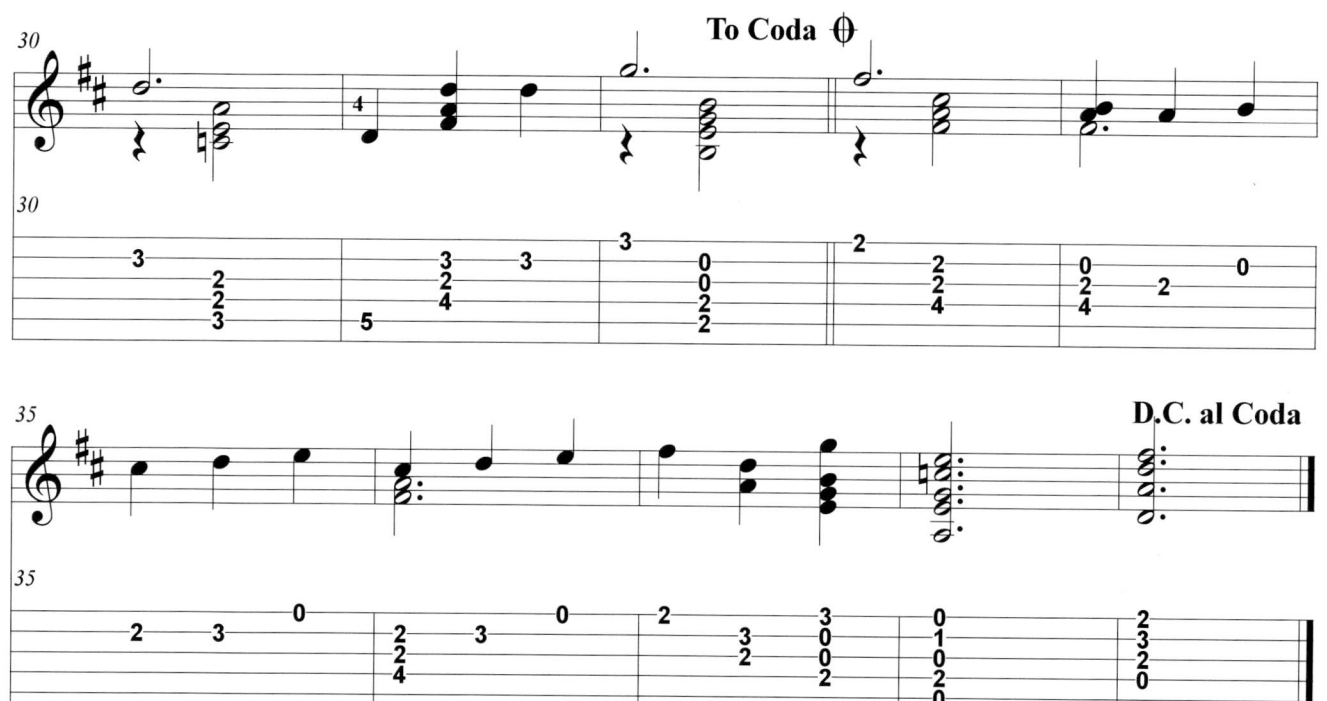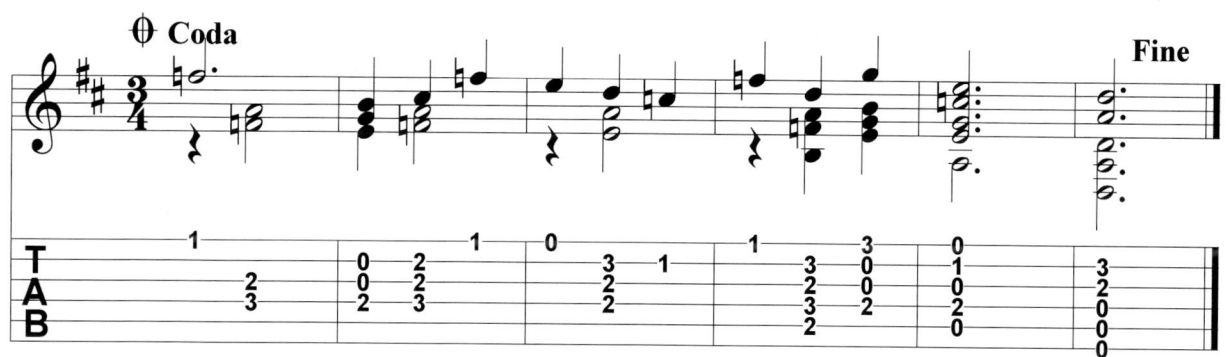

19

Valse

Durand
arr. by Mel Bay

Allegro ♩ = 150

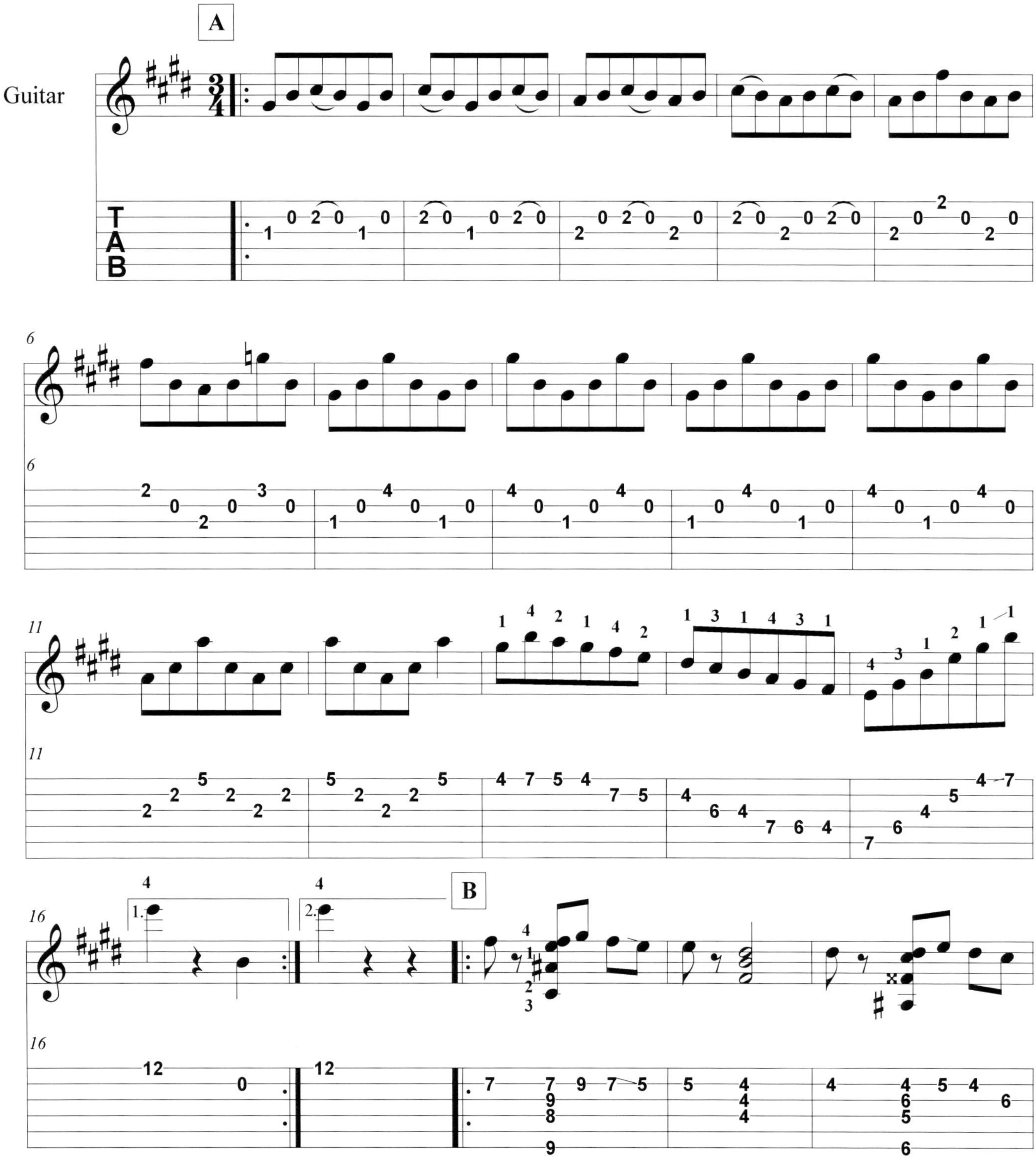

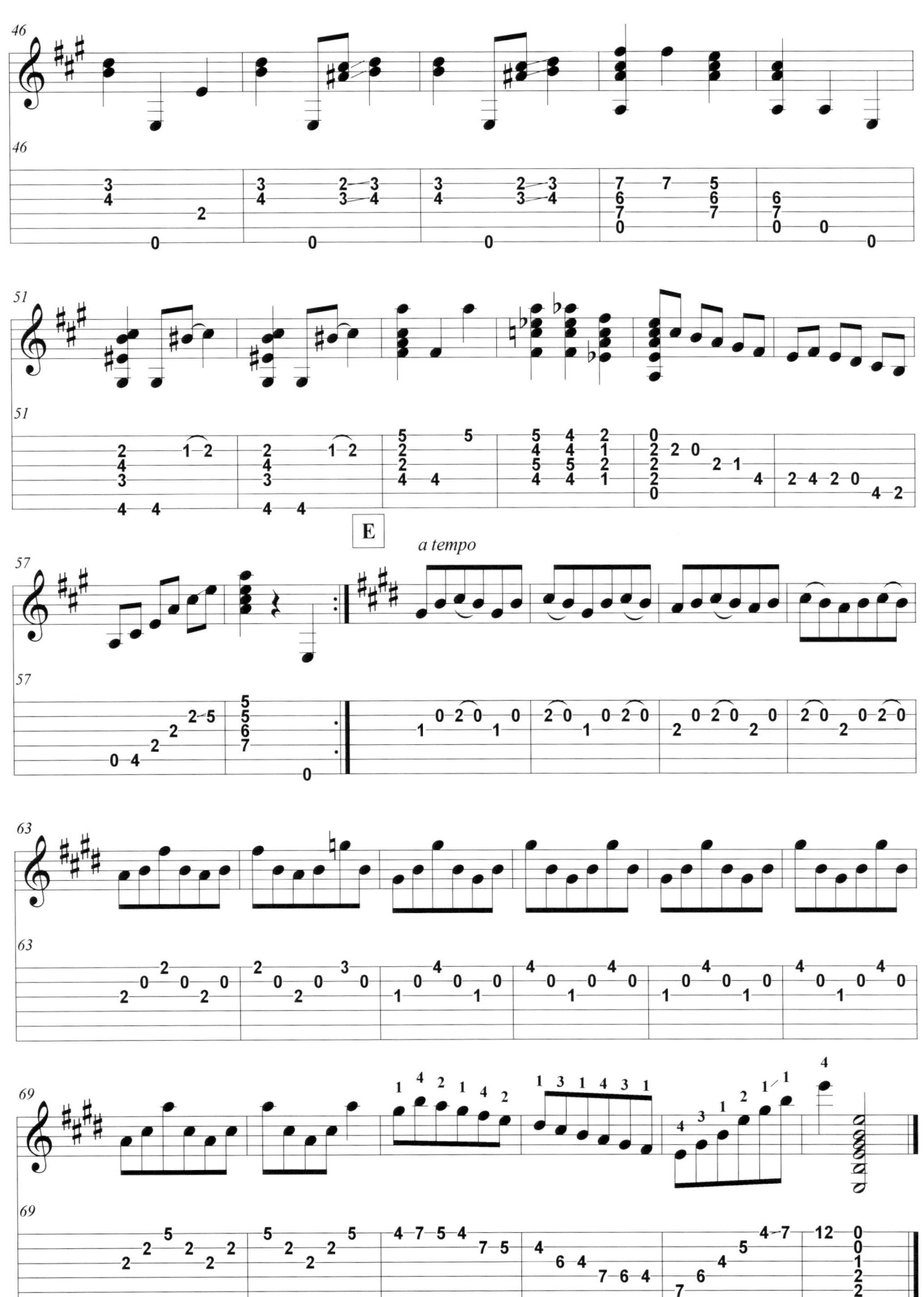

Pavane pour une infante défunte
Theme

Maurice Ravel
arr. by William Bay

Etude

Mozzani
edited by William Bay

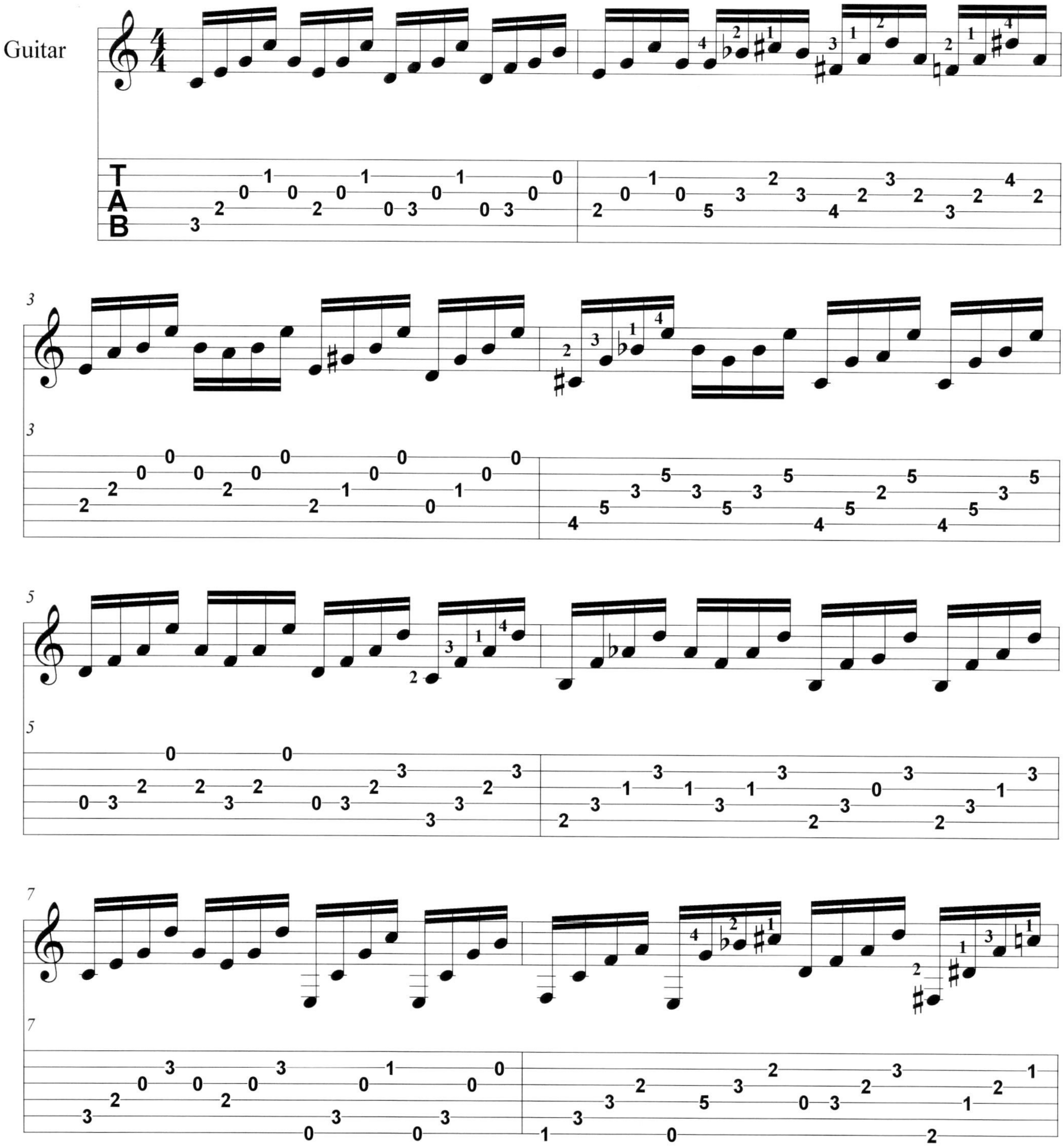

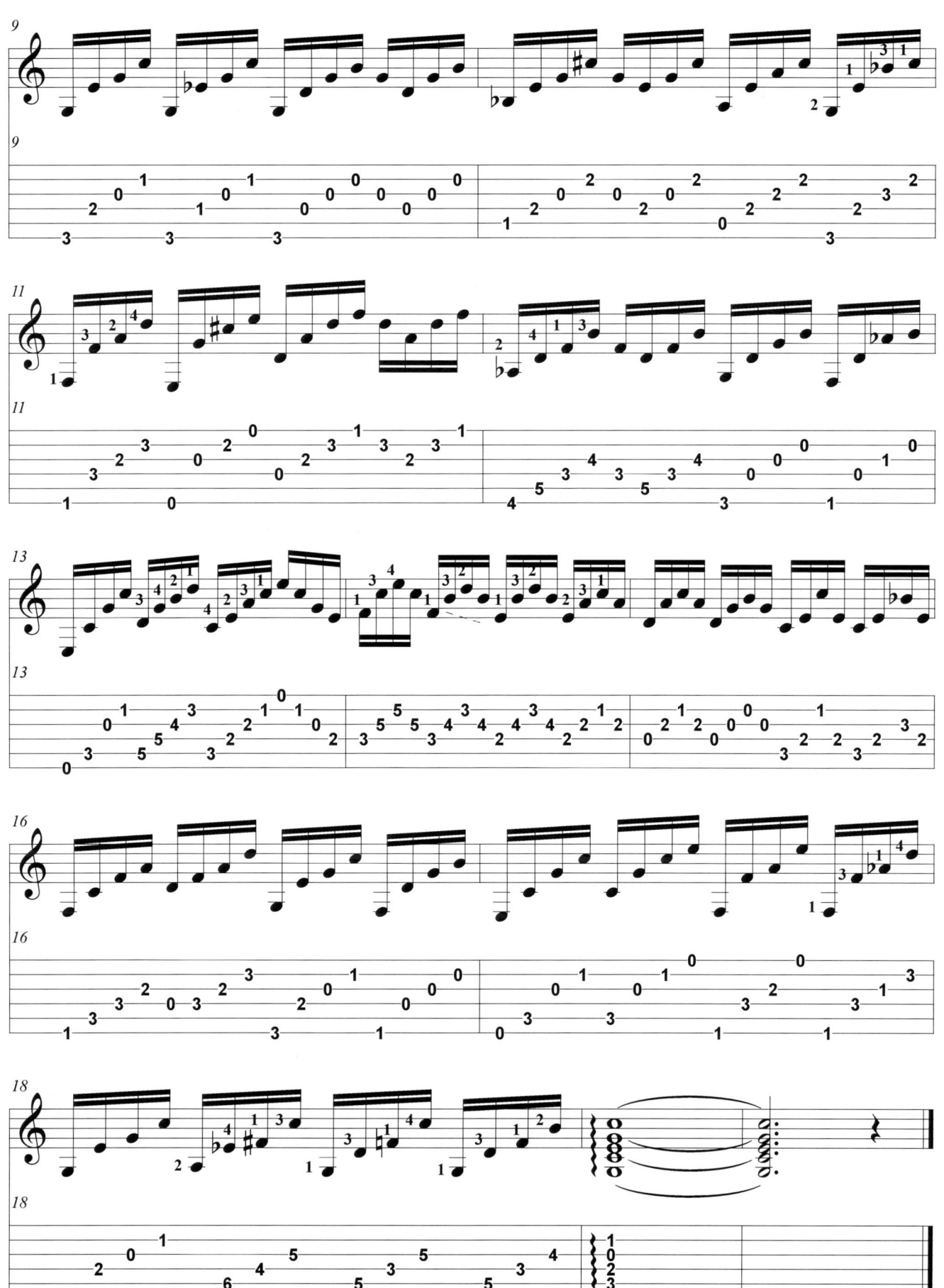

Moonlight Sonata

Beethoven
W.B. based on an arr. by Ray Bell

Dropped-D Tuning

Andante ♩ = 64

Gavotte

J. S. Bach
arr. by Mel Bay

Dropped-D Tuning

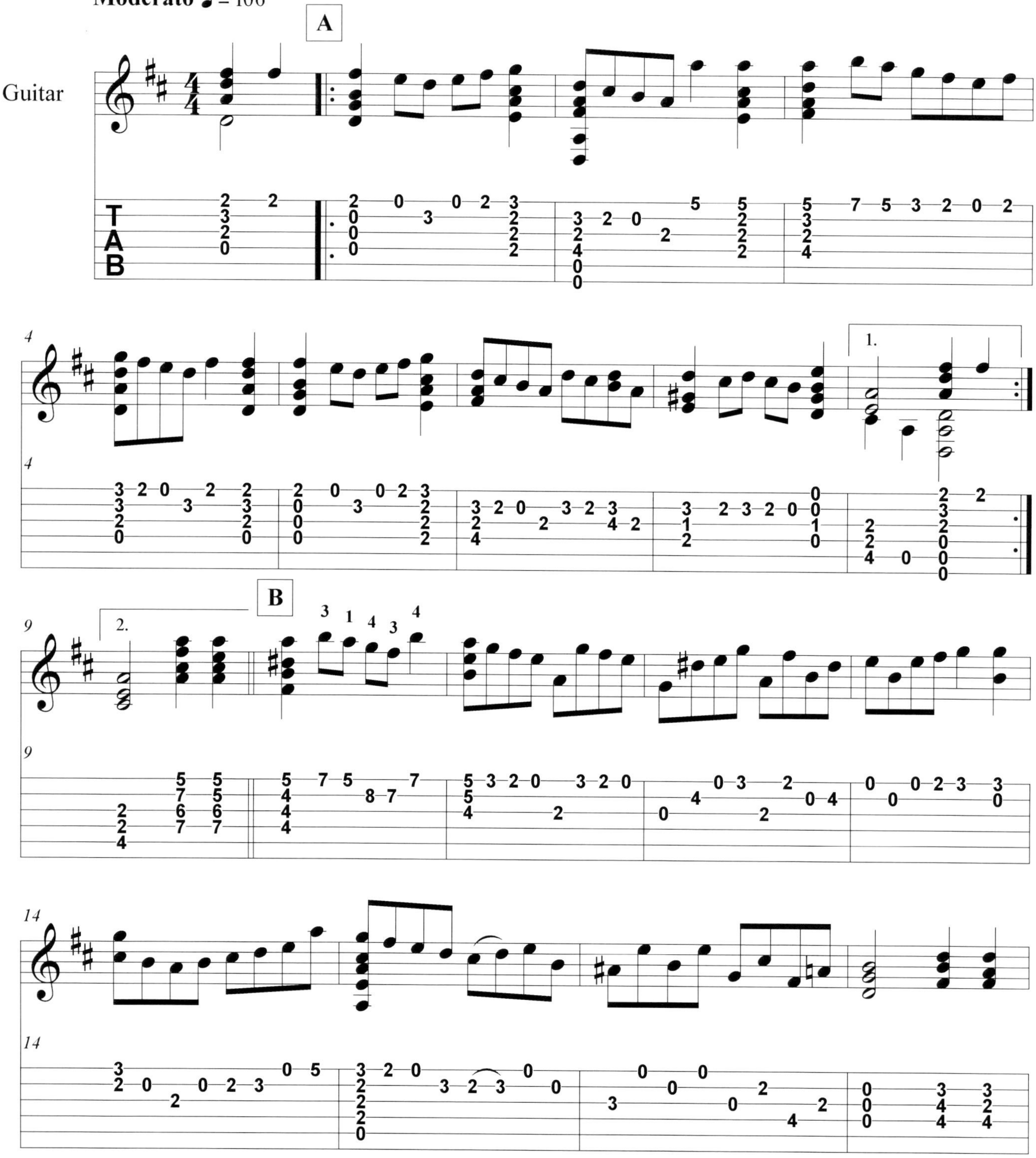

Traumerei

Robert Schumann
arr. by William Bay

Study in D Major

Sor
edited by William Bay

Moderato ♩ = 72

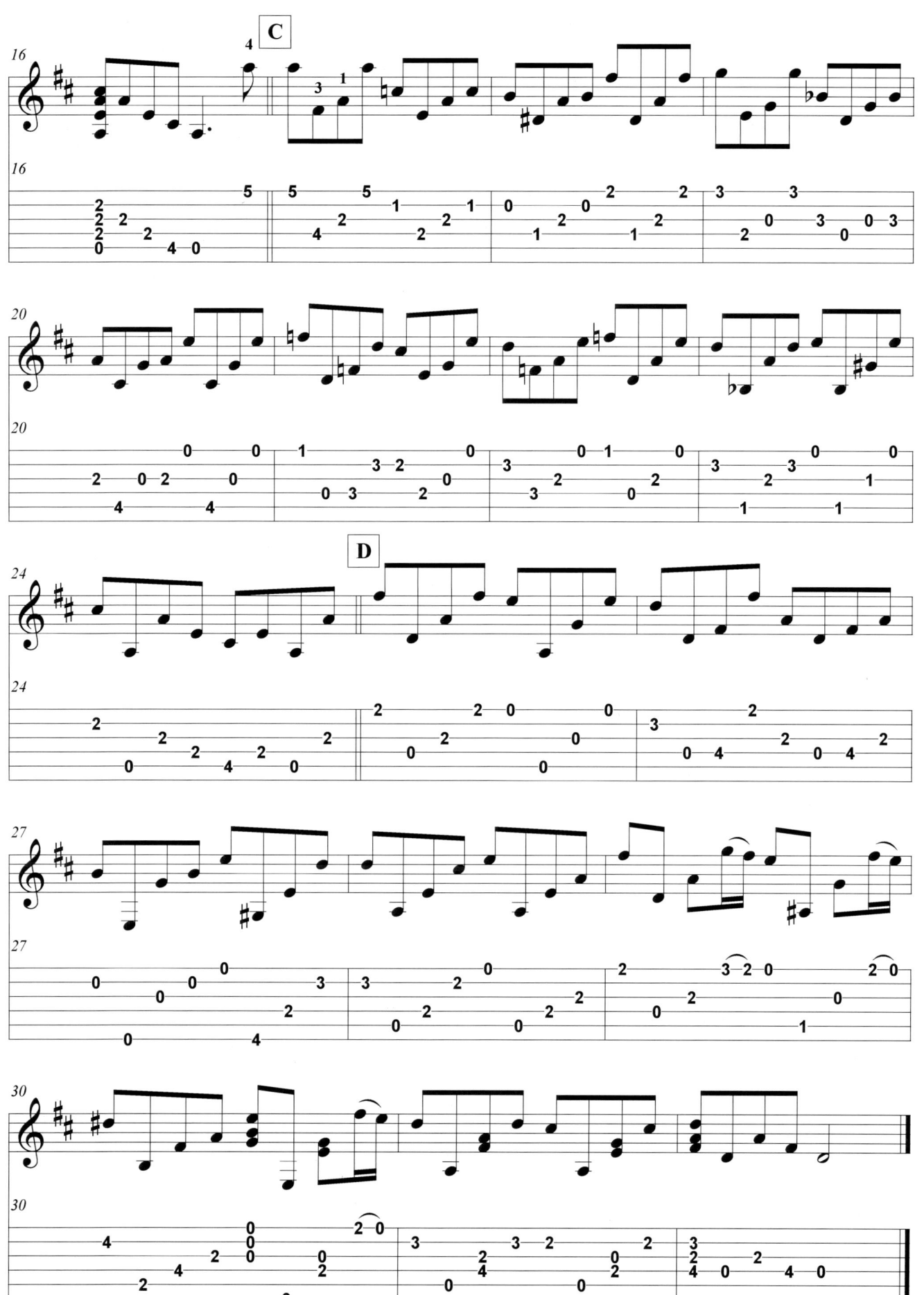

Study in D Minor

Francisco Tárrega
edited by William Bay

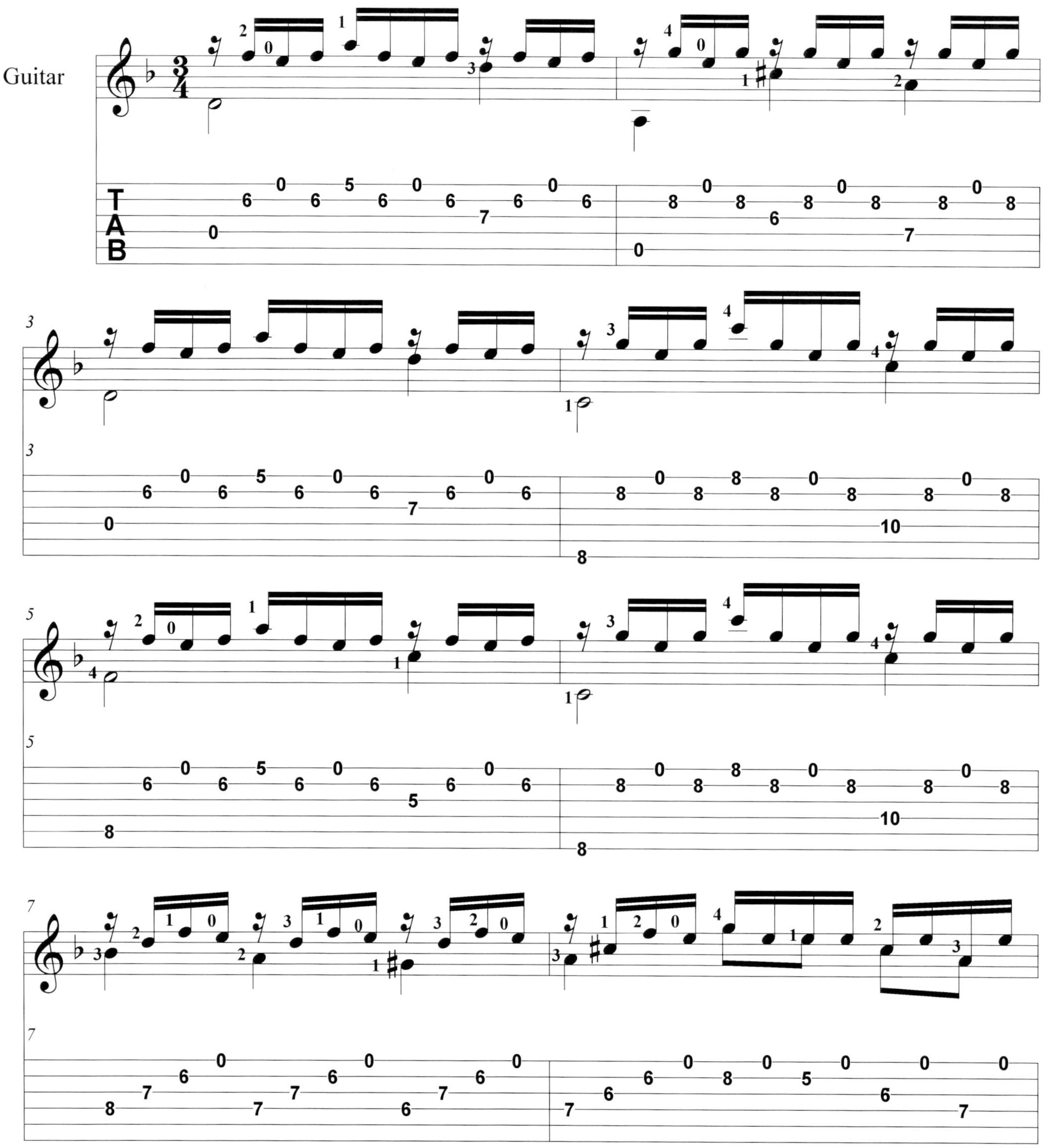

Meditation
From Thaïs

Massenet
arr. by Ray Bell

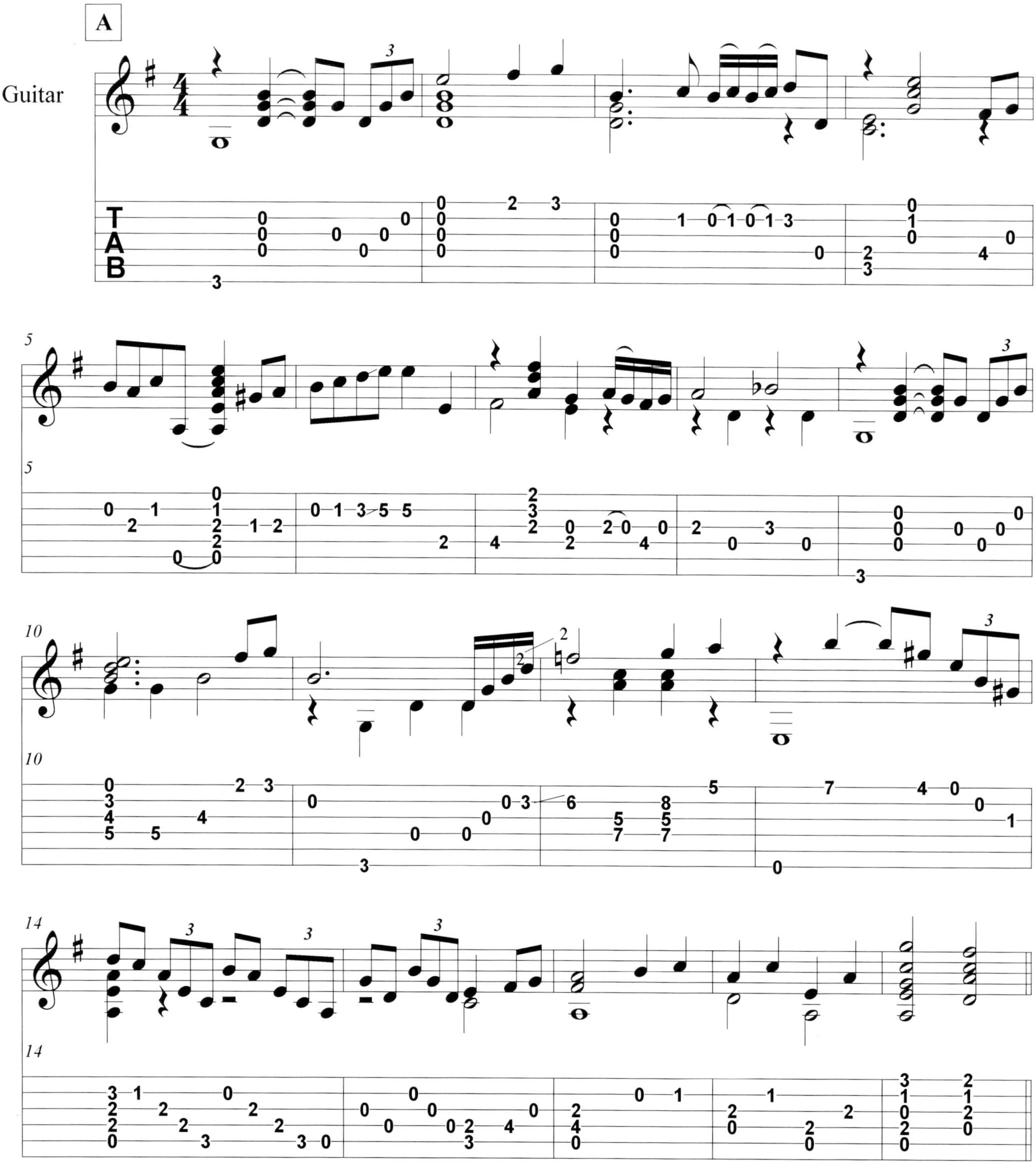

Prelude in B Minor

Sor
edited by William Bay

Largo ♩ = 48

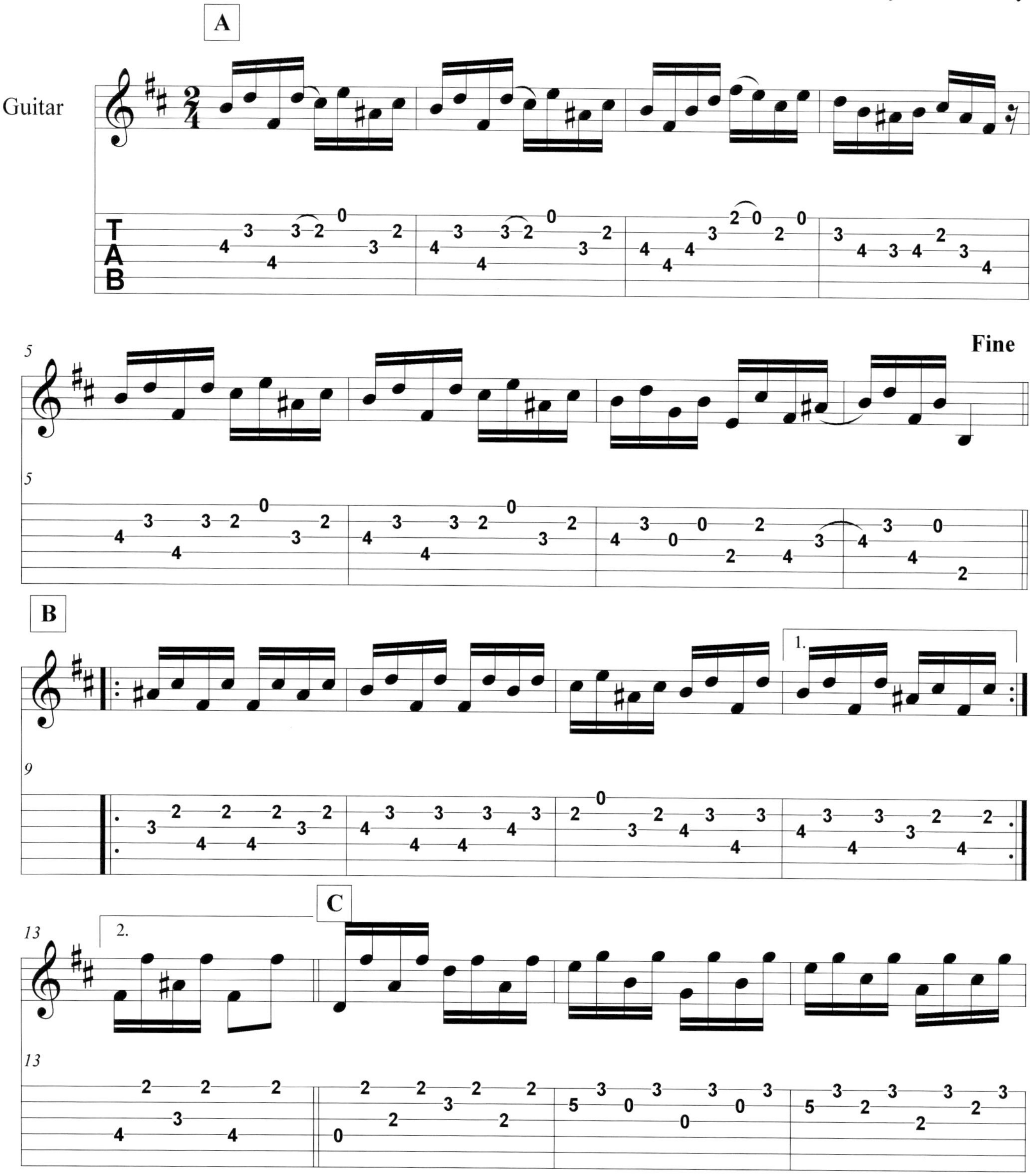

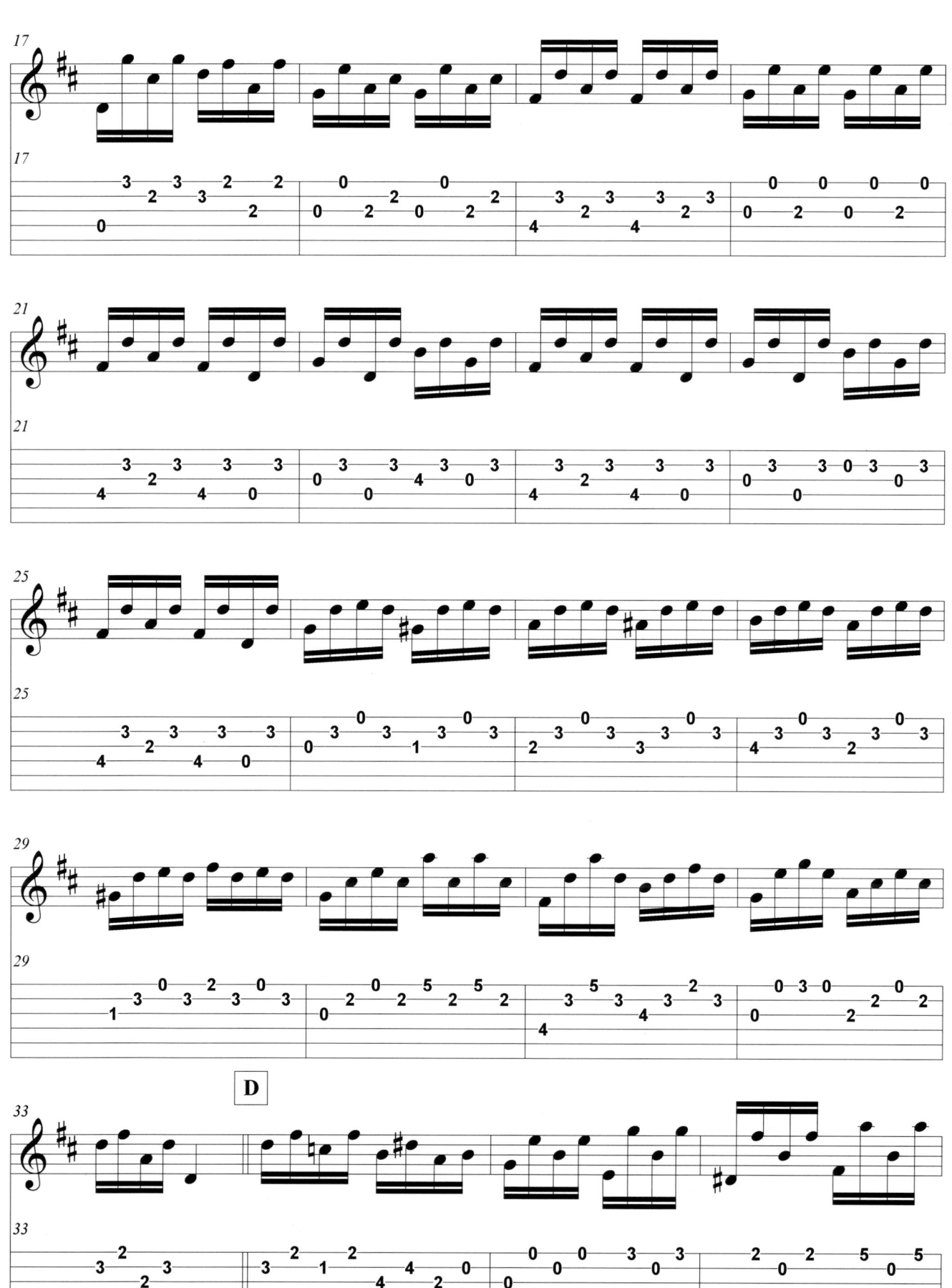

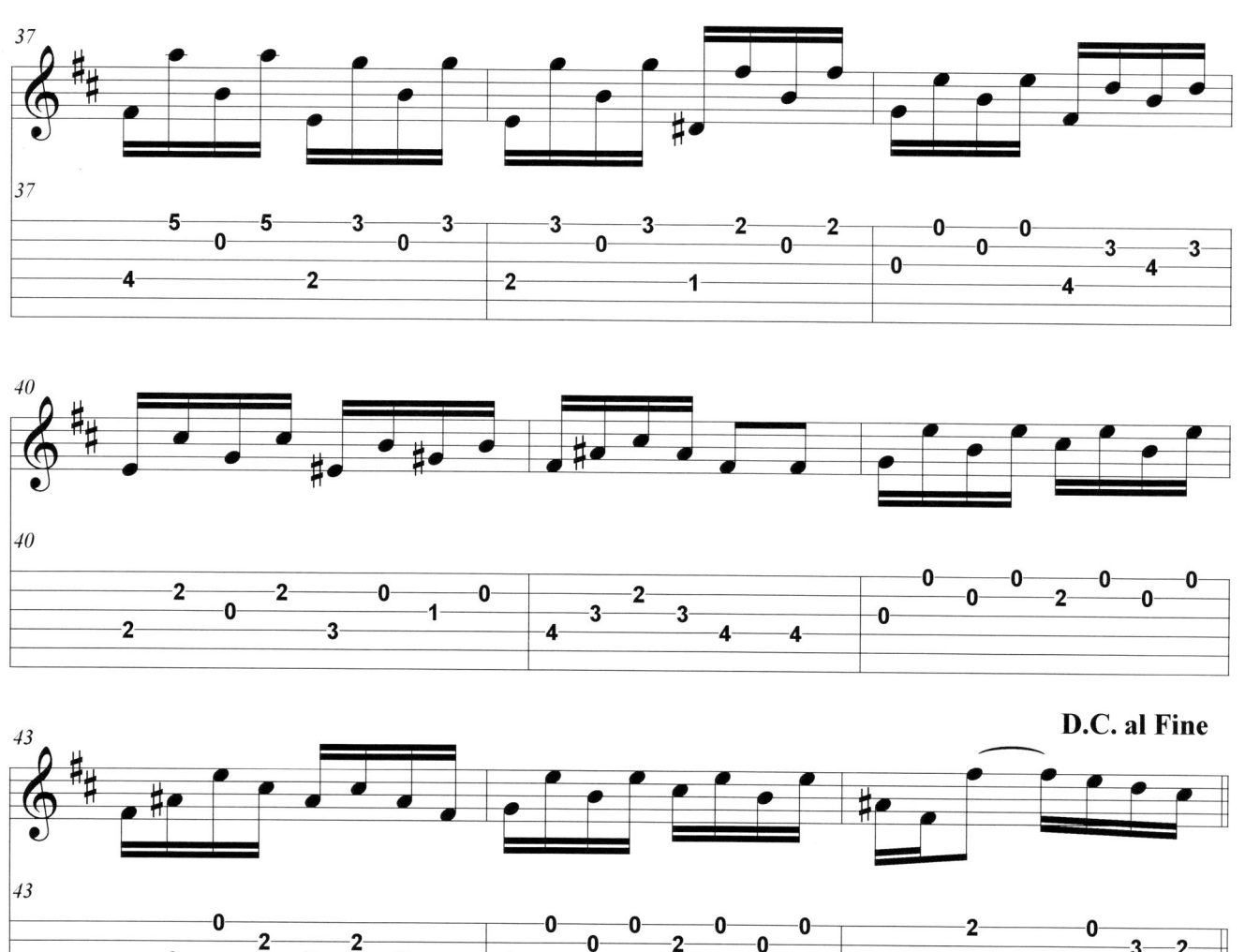

Minuet

Johann Krieger
arr. by William Bay

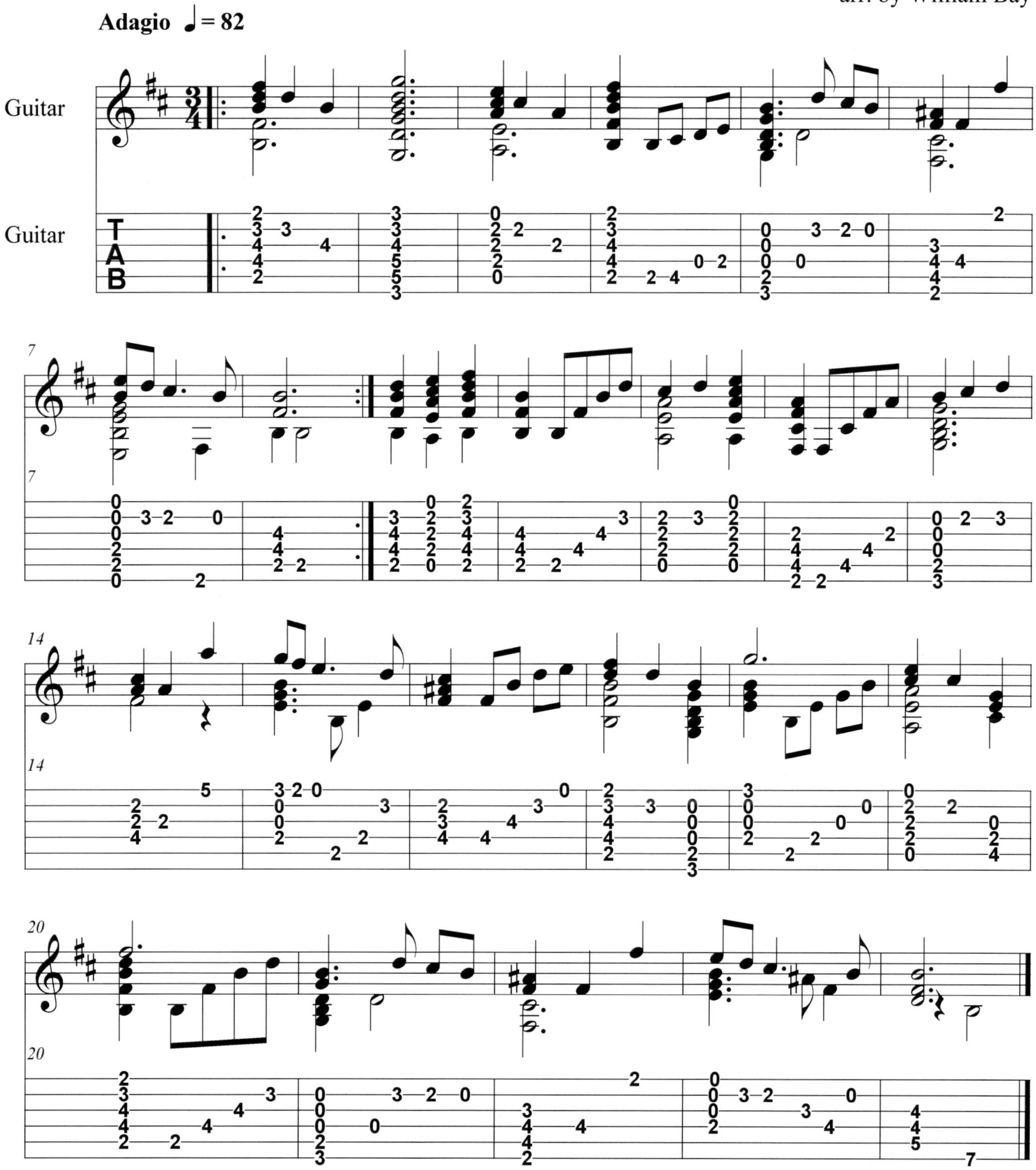

Menuet

Johann Quantz
arr. by William Bay

Andante ♩ = 98

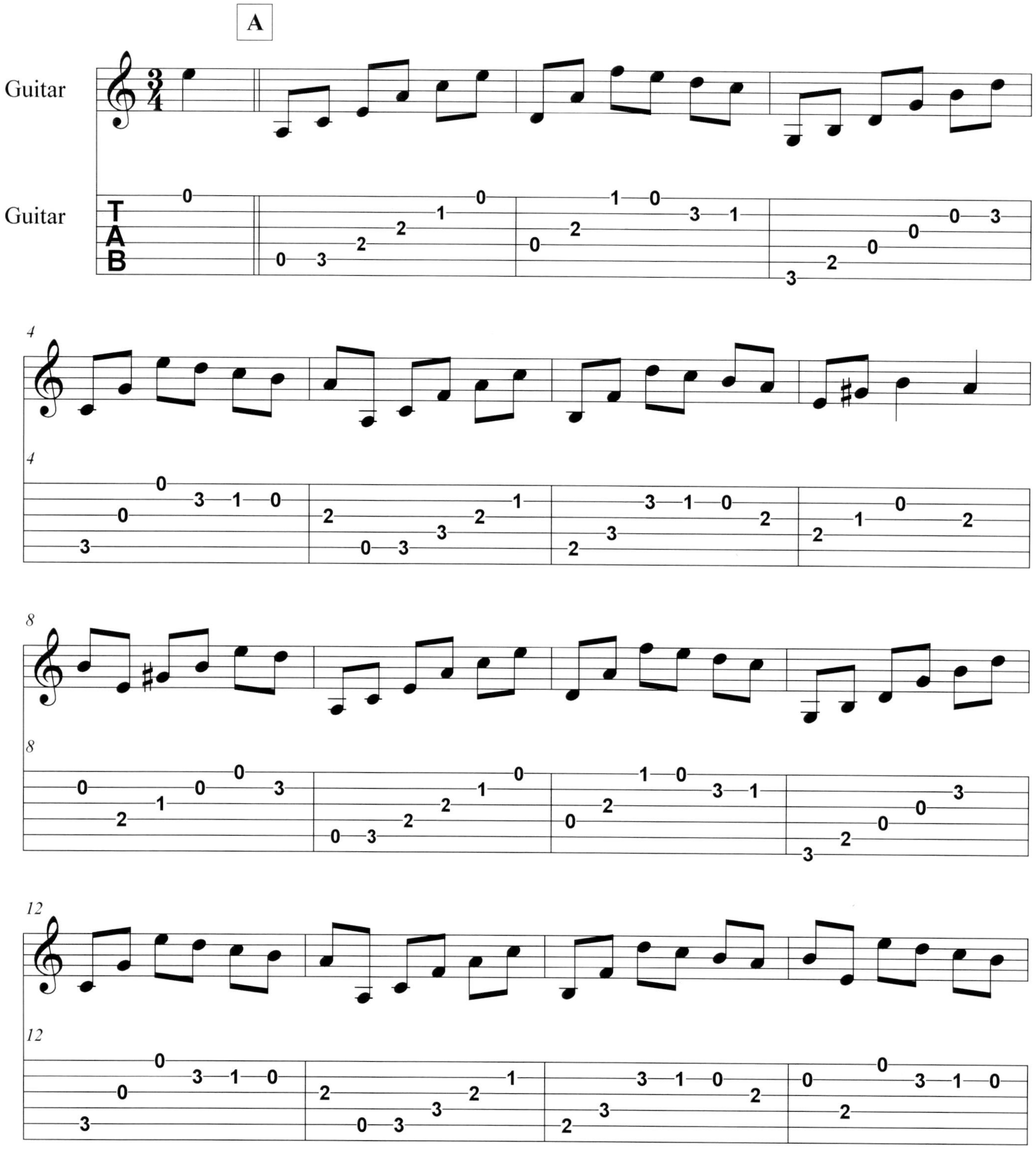

Serenade

Franz Schubert
arr. by William Bay

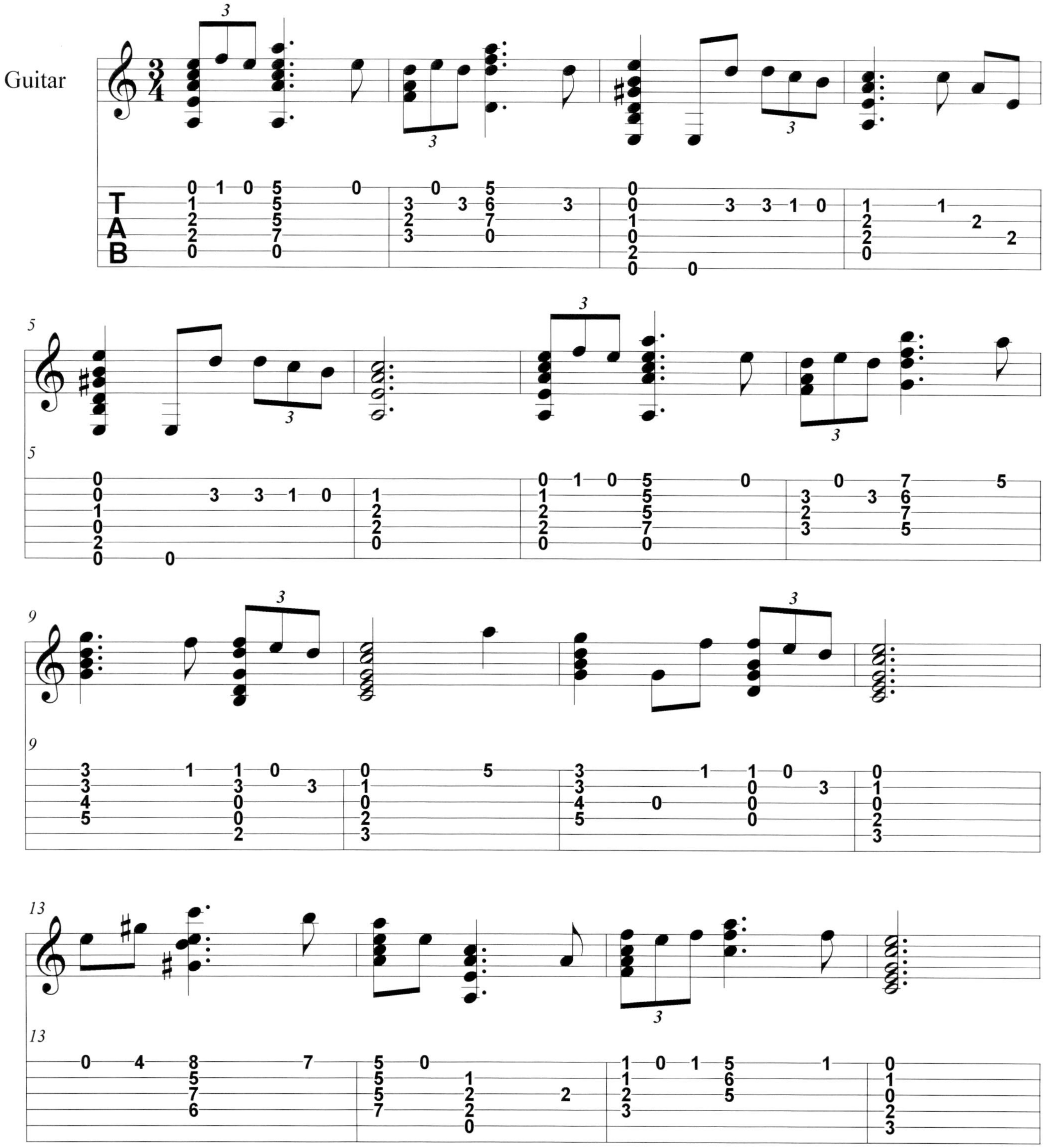

32

The Girl with the Flaxen Hair

Claude Debussy
arr. by Mike Christiansen

Freely ♩ = 68

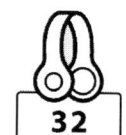

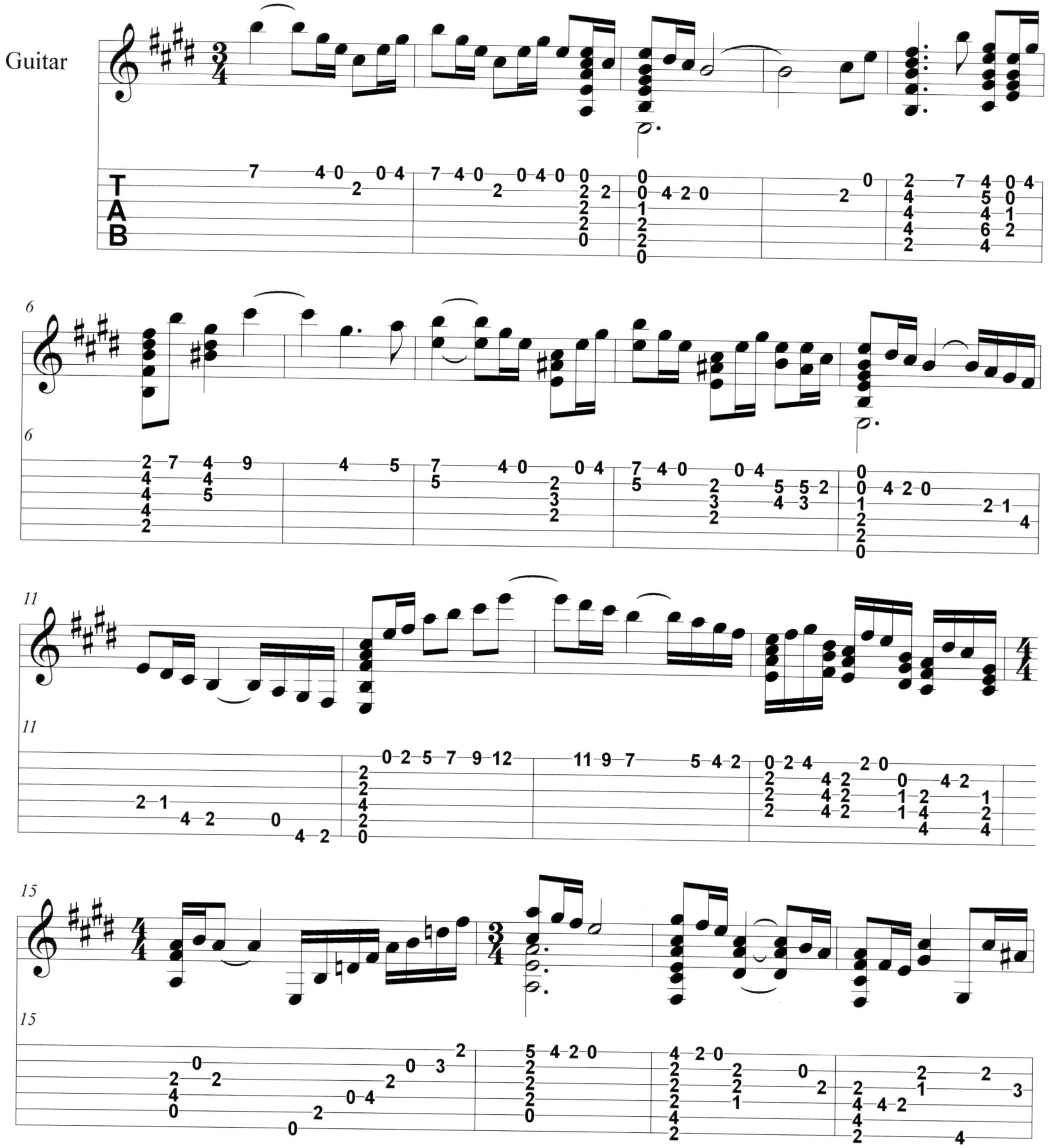

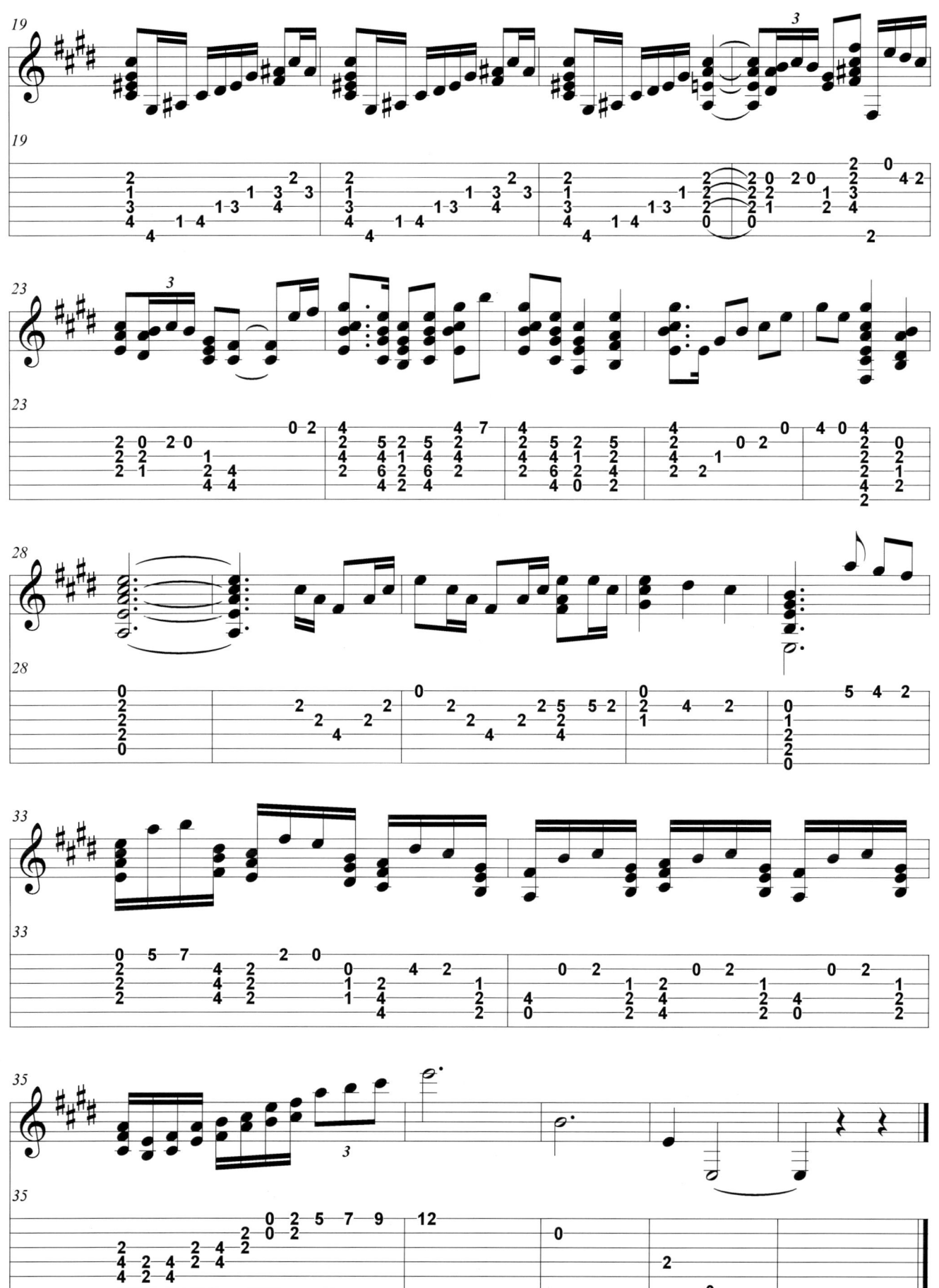

Prelude in C Major

J. S. Bach
edited by William Bay

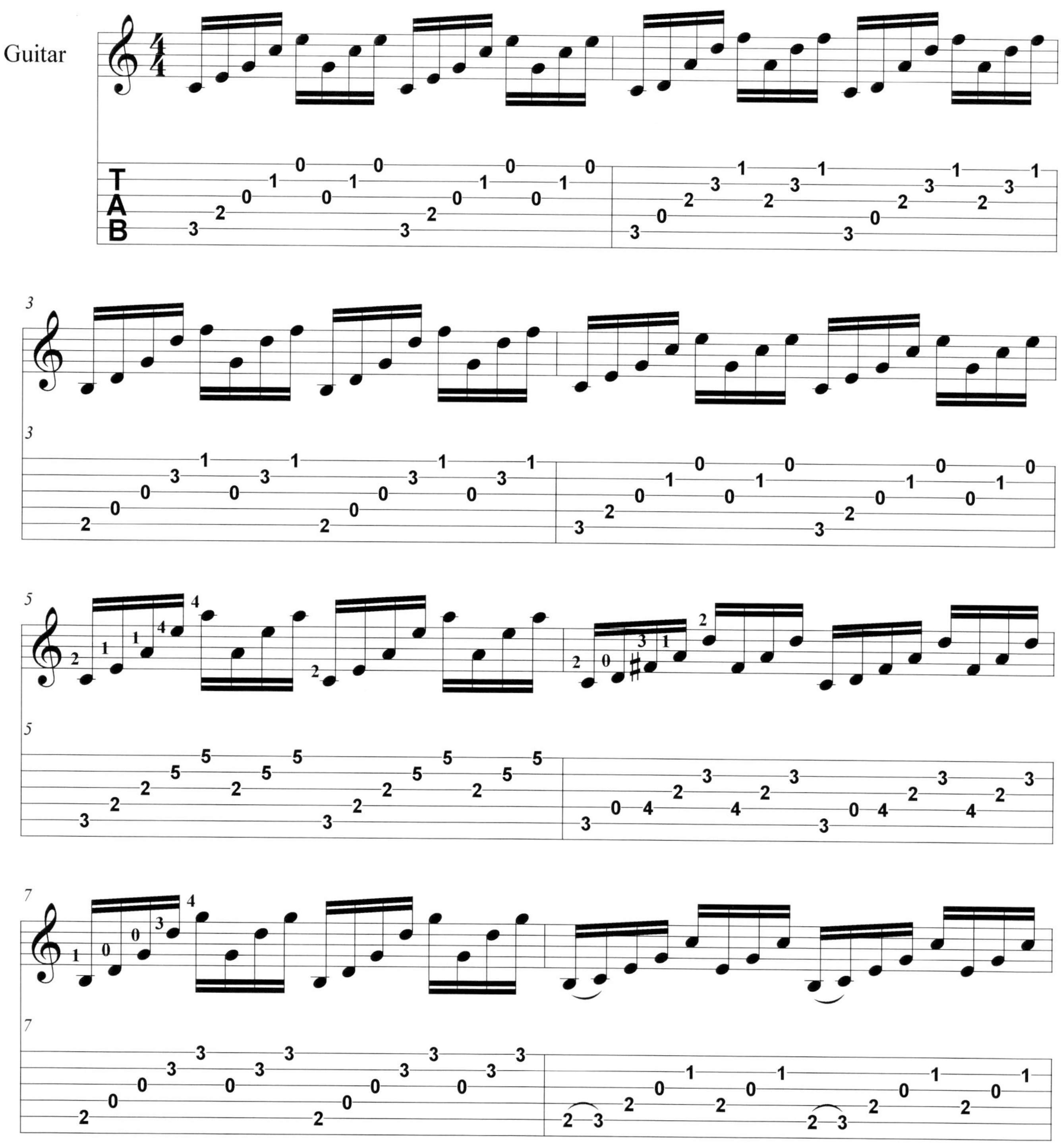

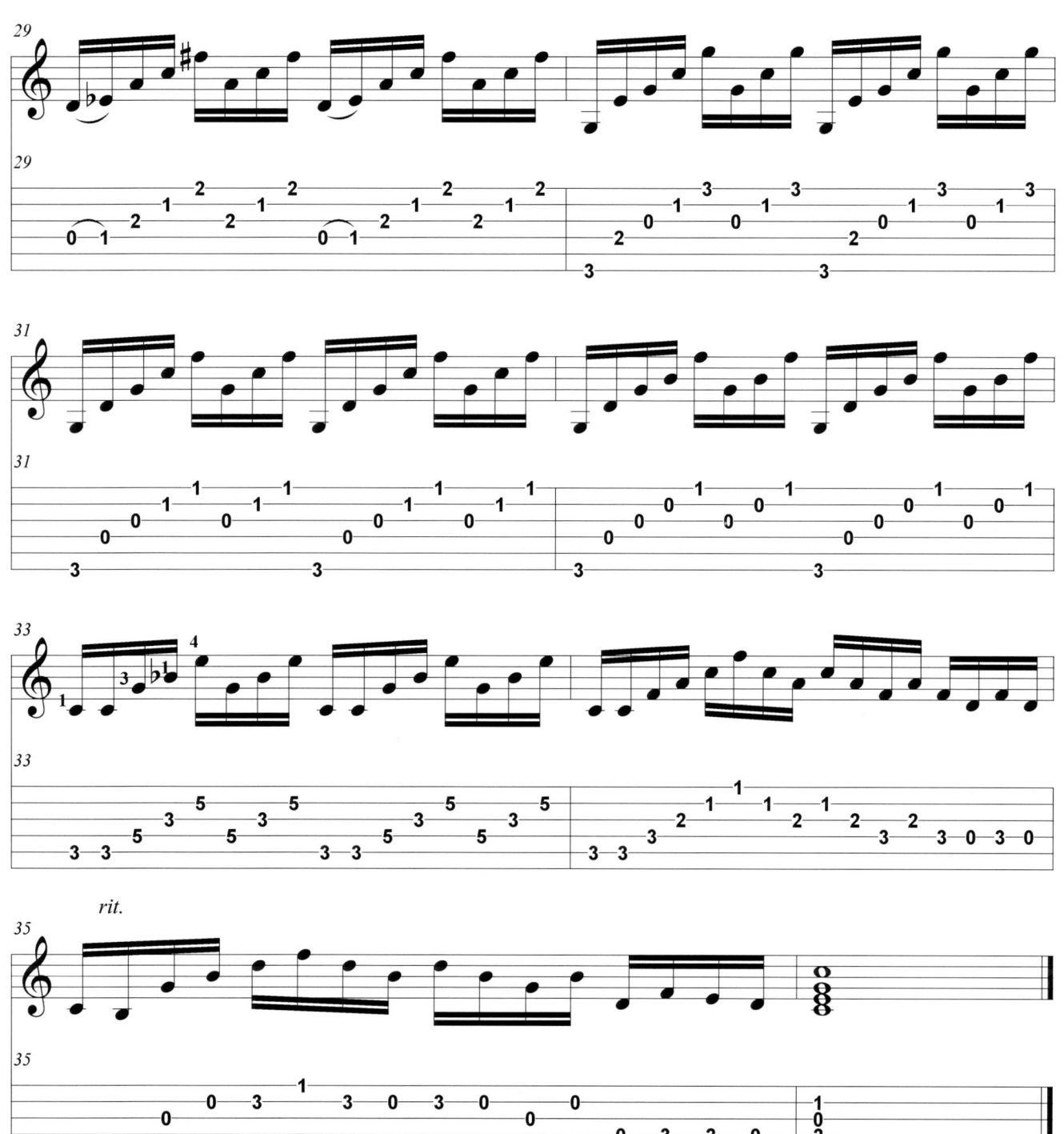

34

La Paloma

Yradier
arr. by Mel Bay

Dropped-D Tuning

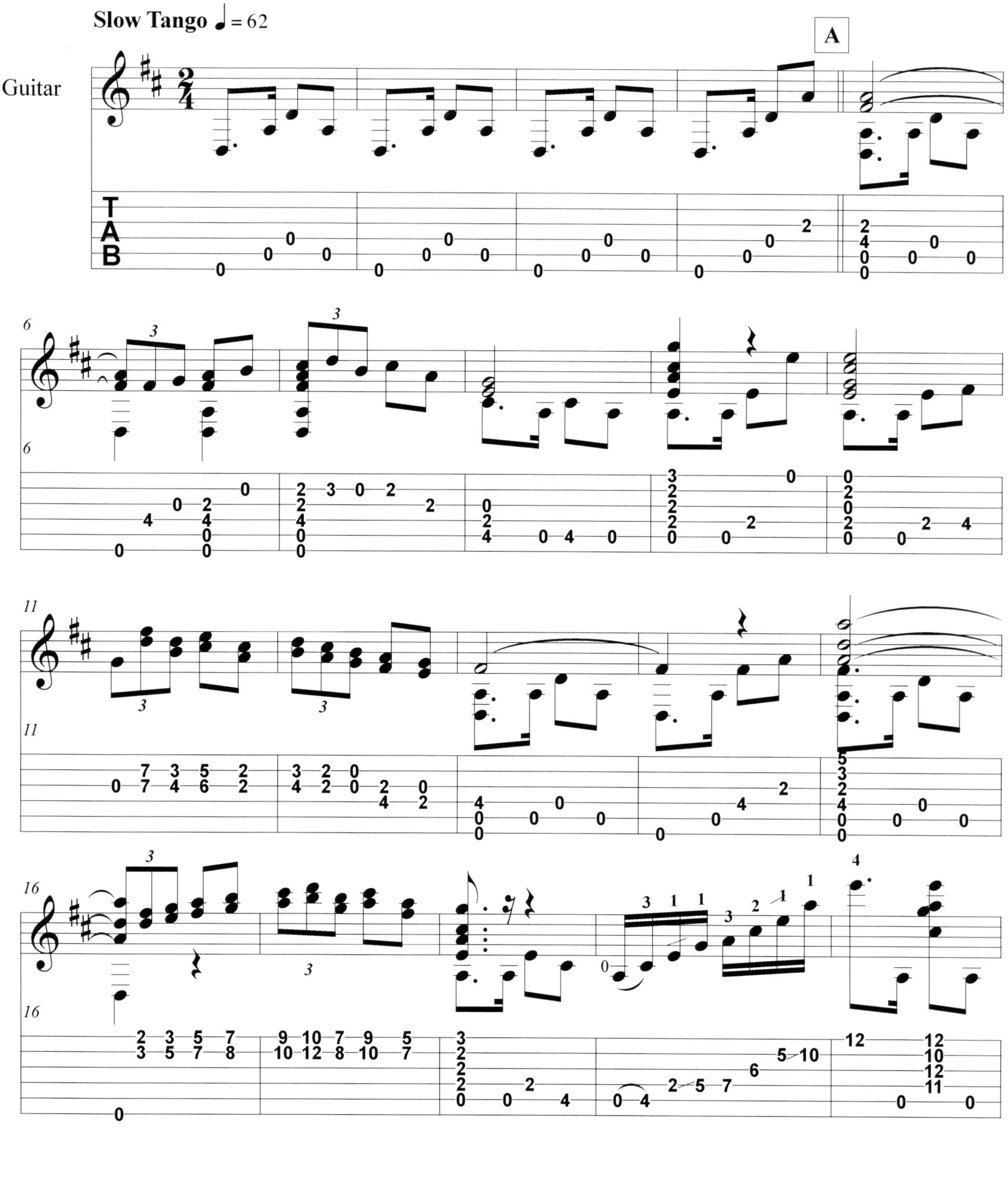

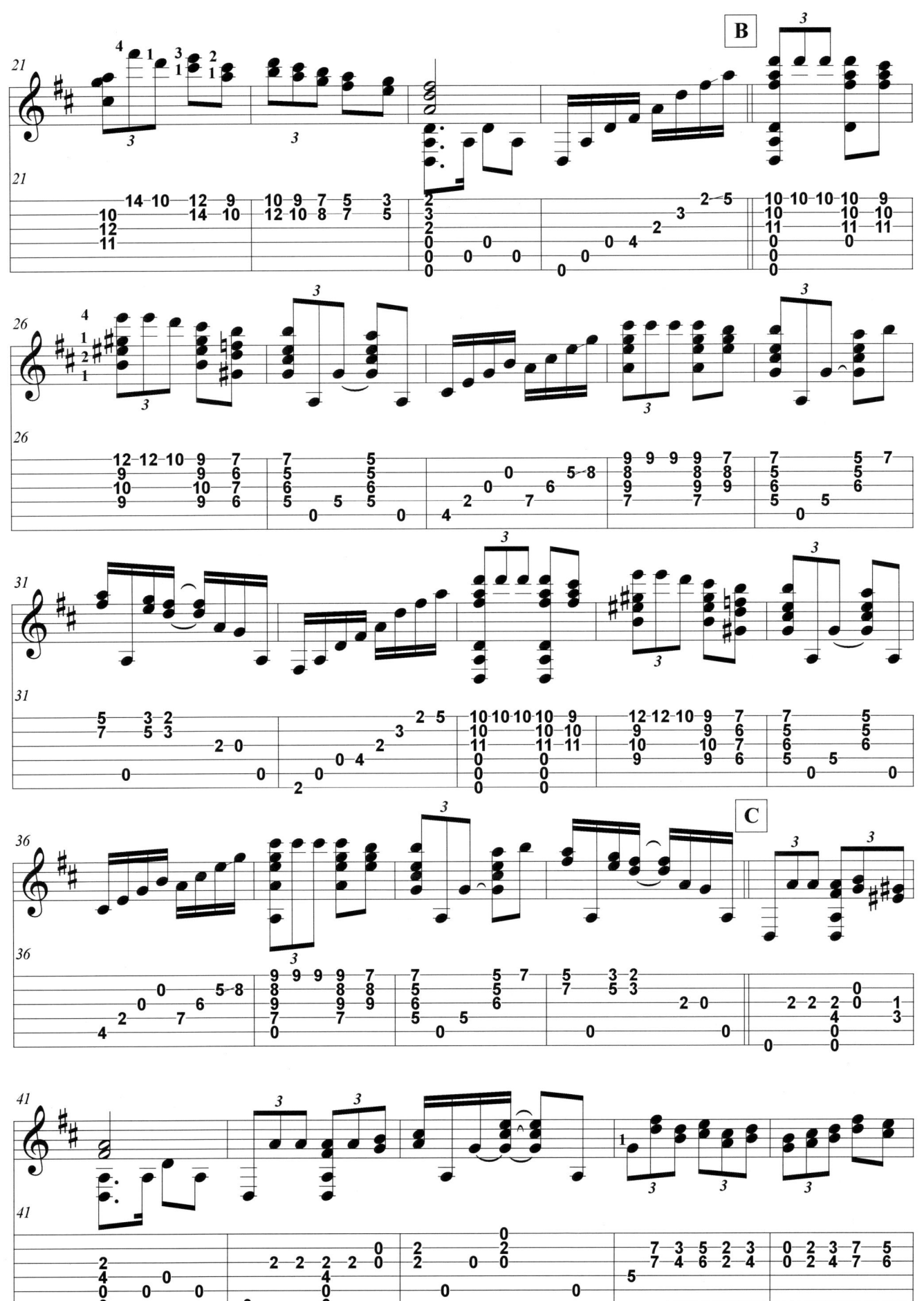

Largo

Dropped-D Tuning

Vivaldi
arr. by William Bay

Slowly ♩ = 72

Acadian Melody

Anonymous
arr. by William Bay

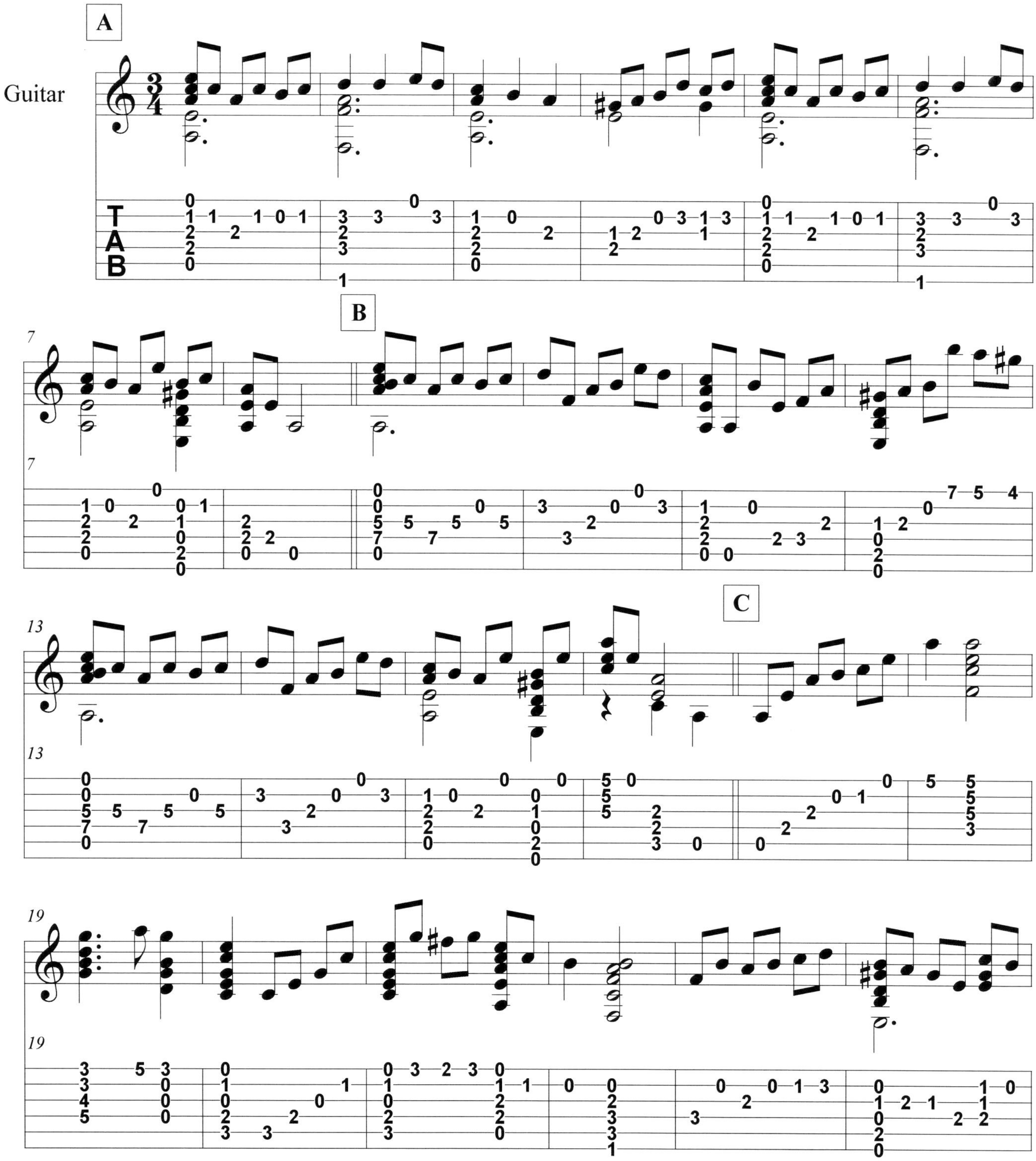

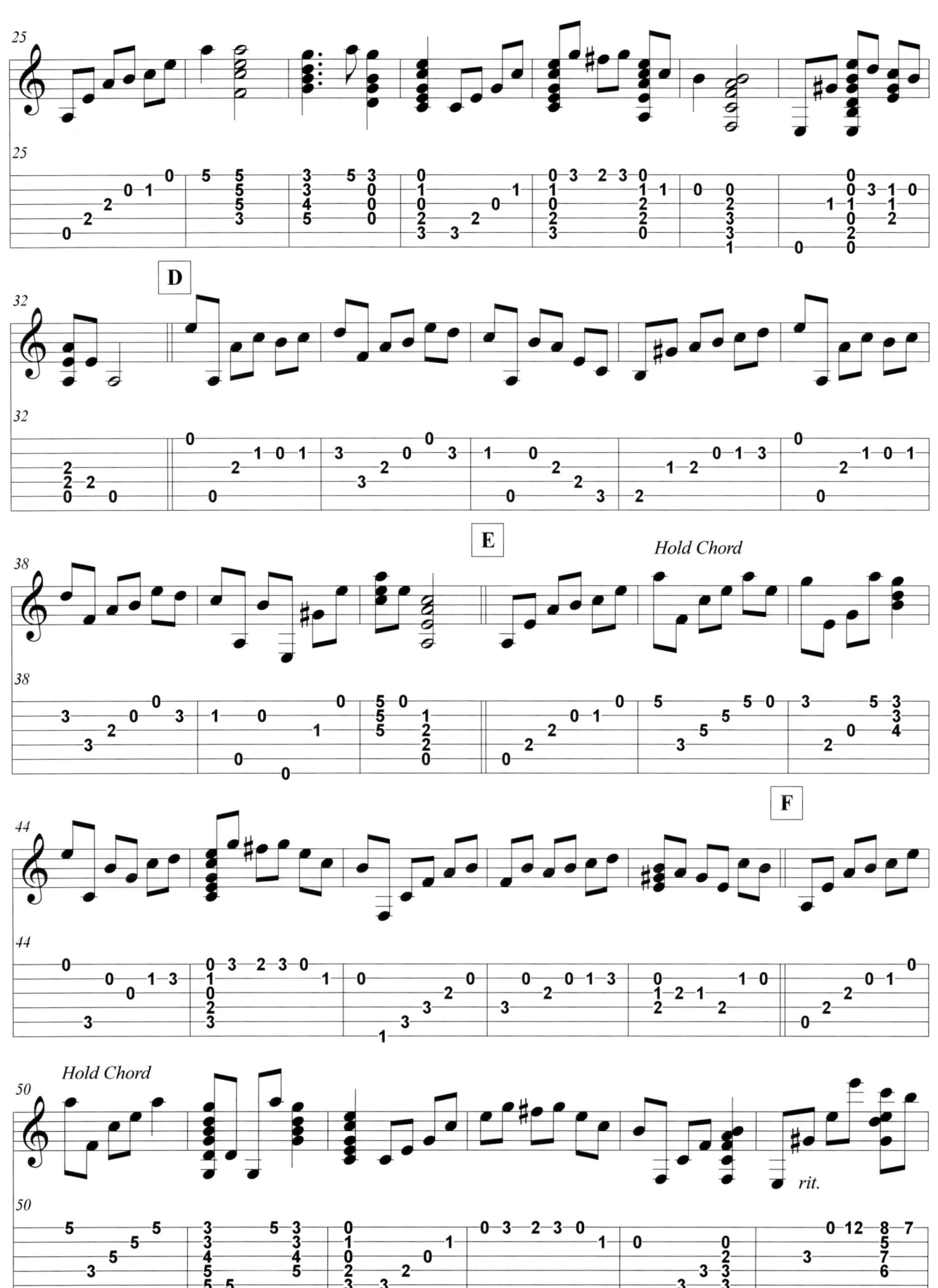